HIKER MIKE

ADVENTURES FARTHER AFIELD

Hey Robin
Get that leg fixed
and get back
on the trail!
Hiker Mike

This book is dedicated
to the memory of
Babu Chiri Sherpa
true friend of
Chomo Lungma

HIKER MIKE

ADVENTURES FARTHER AFIELD

MIKE KIRBY

The BOSTON MILLS PRESS

Cataloguing in Publication Data
Kirby, Mike, 1945–
Hiker Mike : adventures farther afield / Mike Kirby

ISBN 1-55046-392-6

1. Hiking—Guidebooks. 2. Trails—Guidebooks.
I. Title.

GV199.5.K57 2003 796.51 C2002-901542-1

Published in Canada in 2003 by
Boston Mills Press
132 Main Street
Erin, Ontario N0B 1T0
Tel 519-833-2407
Fax 519-833-2195
books@bostonmillspress.com
www.bostonmillspress.com

IN CANADA:
Distributed by Firefly Books Ltd.
3680 Victoria Park Avenue
Willowdale, Ontario M2H 3K1

IN THE UNITED STATES:
Distributed by Firefly Books (U.S.) Inc.
P.O. Box 1338, Ellicott Station
Buffalo, New York 14205

Design: PageWave Graphics

The publisher acknowledges the financial support of the Government of Canada through the Book Publishing Industry Development Program (BPIDP) for its publishing efforts.

Printed and bound in Canada

07 06 05 04 03 1 2 3 4 5

Contents

Publisher's Note: Metric and Imperial measurements are used interchangeably in this book because HM doesn't like to get bogged down in the details, and the mind, like the body, should stay flexible.

Foreword

Hanging by my fingernails on an impossible climb, I thought I had reached the end of my options. I had clambered up an icy ridge, made the mistake of not planning my ascent, and found myself with no way up — and no way down. Just as I was starting to think I was in deep trouble, there was Hiker Mike, not 10 feet above me, salvation in hand.

"Grab this stick," he yelled down the gap, through the howling wind.

Now the decision to put one's life in the hands of a fellow hiker is a fairly easy one. Mike and I had survived six years of hiking together in all kinds of impossible situations, and I knew I could count on him. Without a second thought (okay, maybe one), I reached for the proffered stick, launched myself for the distant handhold and held my breath during that swing across the 200-foot drop. Time stood still for me.

Trust, two hands and a length of wood.

Miraculously, I landed safely and we scrambled to the top, collapsing with laughter at the close call. This was just one of many scrapes I have had since I have been hiking with Mike: the soakers in icy rivers, tumbling down slopes when the rotting tree grabbed for turned into nothing but dust, running from territorial dogs and 'gators, reaching the tops of countless hills with barely the strength left for the final push — all with laughter and camaraderie.

My attraction to this hiking gig has always been its effect on my mind. As a songwriter, I use the time on the trail to compose music. The rhythm of the stride and the breathing lead to ideas that are launched from two active minds not settling for the mundane. This is why I hike with Hiker Mike. He is an endless source of great stories and wonderful philosophy. "Yes to Everything" (from the *Hiker Mike Handbook of Life*) has now become my mantra, and life is simply better with that outlook.

I'm sure that other people find me quite simple-minded when they ask me where we have hiked. Normally I have no idea where we are. Typically we will head off to our hiking trails early in the morning, when we have carved out some time in our busy lives to "sneak out the side door."

Mike always has the plan — he knows how to get to the next adventure. We ride, we talk, and then we get out of the car and walk. It's Mike's overview that gets us there and back — I just walk and sing to myself and try to keep up. I know we have hiked all of the rivers in the Toronto area. We have hiked every inch of our section of the Bruce Trail. We have trekked across the frozen lakes of Temagami and Algonquin. We have scaled Mount Regis in the Adirondacks and soaked ourselves in 'gator-infested Everglades National Park in South Florida, and through it all, managed to come home healthy, happy and relatively unscathed.

It has been a privilege to be included in Hiker Mike's adventures; it has changed my life. Read this book and it will change yours too.

David Bradstreet

HOW IT ALL BEGAN: The "Begin Already" Overview

This book was originally to have been called *25 One-Day Hikes and One 25-Day Hike*, describing my adventures here in the Megacity on a variety of contrasting park, ravine and waterfront trails, leading up to, and preparing for, my 25-day journey from Kathmandu, Nepal, to the Base Camp of Mount Everest at 18,000 feet. This is where climbers from all over the world begin their ascent on the now somewhat sullied and badly abused flanks of the Earth Mother herself, Chomo Lungma.

But the damnable project got away on me. What had begun as a daily journal of my climbing trek from the lowland terraces of rice and potato fields in the Terai Lowlands, up through the pine and rhododendron forests of the Himalayan Foothills, into the Solo Khumbu Valley (home of the one-time nomad Sherpa nation), and thereby achieving the high Himalaya, by way of the Khumbu Glacier and the Icefall, turned into a rather large amount of information, judging by the length of this sentence, that simply would not fit into the back half of the proposed *Farther Afield* book. And so the Everest journey must wait to see the inside of the bookstore travel section until a later date, and now we can return to the project at hand.

Here, inside, you will find a few dozen fat Megacity warm-up hikes, varying in length and degree of difficulty, that will prepare us to then get the hell out of town to exotic hiking locales in "strands afar remote," beginning with an Algonquin–Adirondack Adventure section, wherein we will explore not only the guts of the wilderness interiors, but also the Frontenac Trail that connects the two. Bet you didn't know that an Algonquin-to-Adirondack Trail was being developed, did you? Well, now you do and you're finding out about it not too long after me. So welcome to the ever-changing, brave new world of hiking.

Farther Afield also contains numerous Q-and-A's from Hiker Mike's pen pals from around the world, in which we will be informed about hiking trails and outdoor gear, and will hear tall tales and reminiscences by good people who took the time to shoot me cyber notes from all over North America. We'll also take a trip down memory trail to Temagami Red Pine Ridge, overlooking the mystical White Bear Old Growth Forest.

Then, moving well out of Ontario, we will wing our way west to Vancouver, where we will hike the Coast Mountains around the city, starting, and almost ending, with the bastard hike, the Grouse Grind, in which Hiker Mike attempts the impossible under the influence of half a joint of Island bud. It's just one of a half dozen or so spectacular psychedelic hikes from Cypress Bowl past Squamish's "The Chief" and on up the Sea to Sky Highway to Whistler's Black Tusk and the glacier lake, Garibaldi. We will finish our epic journey with a week's worth of restful and recuperative hiking on the amazing out island of Bahama's Great Exuma, where taximan Kermit Rolle and the naked hermit Hanno will show us the ocean, jungles and beaches of the world's most beautiful coral island in the Gulf Stream. Be there or be a wussy, baby!

I will make sure that you will enjoy following in the Hiker's footsteps, if you decide to go yourself, by giving specific directions on how to find the people and places that actually exist and helped me on my way, as they will you. I will make mention of guest houses, state parks, campsites, restaurants, brothels, and most important, directions to the trailheads that are waiting for you, that is, if you decide to rise up off your big, fat, lazy and ever-expanding butt. Or you may carry on doing what you're doing and read my expedition accounts during the commercial breaks of that *National Geographic* special that you're watching for exercise. Either way, you'll be getting out there and exploring the Big Blue Ball we call Earth, even if you only dream of one day hitting that Comeback Trail to Fitness. Just imagine yourself with both feet firmly planted in a pair of light hiking boots, map and compass in hand and that familiar old escapist grin breaking out all over your face.

ADVICE TO THE BOOTLESS

1 *Big Fat Porky Bum*

In 1978, I was diagnosed with rheumatoid arthritis in my left hip, which the doctor said would get potentially worse and increasingly painful as I ventured down the road of life and into the wheelchair. So, ever the contrarian, going against the grain as it were, I started running 20 minutes or so and worked my way up to an hour a day, for over 10 years. And now, some 20-plus years later, I am hiking 5 miles a day with no more arthritic symptoms.

Boomer's hips are in the news these days. Joints can be replaced, but it takes years to get them back to full use. Or you can start walking today for a few minutes and working your way through the creaks and bangs and pain. Our bodies are wonderful instruments, always adjusting to what we throw at them. The body is either evolving and growing or degenerating and dying. So let's make the decision to screw up our courage and get all our joints working again.

Let's start by giving our knees and hips a lube job. When I ran regularly, I always woke up the next day with a sore back, sore knees, and swollen ankles. Now when I hike, I get up the next day feeling grand and proceed to hike again. No pain in the joints, hikers. Just keep it moving down the trail to the grocery store, over to the school to pick up the kids, or up to the park to walk the doggies. We've got to stay flexible. Squat down on your haunches every day. Stay loose. No one wants to end up on the bottom of the bathtub with a busted hip. You'll take

Pen Pal: Dave

"Hi, Hiker Mike, I am going to both Tanzania and Serengeti and climbing Kilimanjaro. I am looking for a boot that can work in both environments. To complicate matters I have wide feet (4E). Any suggestions? Thx."

— *Dave*

"Check out the Dunham Storm Cloud 9, they're leather and waterproof with great traction and so comfy your feet will feel like they're walkin' on marshmallows." — *HM*

a lot of pleasure on the Comeback Trail to Flexibility. Just remember: rigid — bad! flexible — good!

Sometimes the answer is right in front of us. Hiking's not rocket science. It's one foot in front of the other. So let's all get up off our big, fat, porky bums and take a hike for our own flexibility's sake.

2 *Dressing for Cold Weather: Layering and Boots*

Every autumn we move into the cold and wet part of the year, so let's talk about hiking attire: clothing and boots. The secret to comfy hiking is the layering of your clothing. Next to your skin, wear a cotton, long-sleeved turtleneck, covered by a synthetic fleece or wool sweater, then a Gore-Tex shell with a hood for wind and rain — try the LoweAlpine triple ceramic jacket — pricey but good for life. And finally, for those below-zero days, add a light down parka. Make sure the parka covers your butt for sitting around after the hike. There you have it. Cotton, fleece, Gore-Tex and down.

You see, hikers, as you heat up on the trail, you can strip off a layer and stash it in your backpack. Even your down jacket should squinch up into a little ball in the bottom. Always carry some water and some chocolate and take along a change of SmartWool socks to refresh your feet halfway through the hike. Now that you're dressed properly, how about a good sturdy pair of hiking boots. Make them light and fleecy, and wide enough to accommodate all five toes.

I dropped in to see my boot guy, Arnold Tse, who was working the grand opening of the New Balance flagship store at the corner of Yonge and Delisle Streets in Toronto. Arnold had come over to New Balance from Sporting Life and now heads up the technical end of the company, taking care of special clients like marathon runners and mountain climbers. Arnold was eager to introduce me to Clarence Rosevear, the boot guy from Dunham Boots, who had a pair of Green Mountain hightop, lightweight leather hikers with rubber soles.

"Here, Hiker Mike," says Clarence. "Take these Green Mountain hikers out into the bush and beat the living daylights out of them, and bring them back if you find any defects." So I strapped on a pair of 12EEs, thanked him, and hiked out of the store.

Dunham Bootmakers, a division of New Balance, opened for business in 1885 in Battleboro, Vermont, and introduced North America to the first waterproof leather boot, called the Original, and the first alpine hiker, called the Waffle Stomper — light hikers with structure. You can trust the grip to keep from sliding, either up or downhill in all seasons, and in all conditions: ice, mud, dead leaves and snow. And you don't twist ankles when your feet come down on uneven terrain. But most of all, they're light as a feather, like barefoot hiking, especially when this day-tripper dilettante ain't carrying a backpack. And I hate backpacks. Without one, I can walk 25 miles a day, have some dinner and a good night's sleep and start out next morning hiking — pain and stiffness free.

I do think I've found the boot to replace those Salomons I've been wearing out. I gave the Green Mountain hikers every opportunity to get soaked in the cedar swamps of the Oak Ridges Moraine. The leather uppers on the outside of the boot were submerged clear to the laces, but I didn't feel any moisture inside the boot. Know why? 'Cause they're damnably waterproof!

I checked when I got home. I took them off, shoved my hand inside, and found a webbed layer of fabric between the leather and my foot that won't let the water through. Now the Dunham

Pen Pal: Gay McCreath: Polypro good! Cotton bad!

"I was listening to you this morning and was surprised to hear you recommend cotton next to the skin while hiking. My husband and I are experienced hikers from Orillia and have always understood that cotton underwear should be avoided. Cotton holds the moisture and does not dry quickly, leading to hypothermia. In fact in the mountain areas such as the Adirondacks and White Mountains, they post warnings saying 'Cotton Kills.' What is usually recommended is some type of polypropylene. It wicks the moisture from your skin, dries fast and is very comfortable and warm. Not trying to dispute your advice but wondered if you know something that we don't." — *Gay McCreath*

"You're absolutely right! For long and arduous hikes, polypro is probably best. But I find that after a good strong day hike, I start to stink in polypro. Don't ask me why, but I find cotton allows my body to breath so much better than synthetics. Besides, cotton is sooooo comfy next to my skin." — *HM*

Pen Pal: Irene Rosso

"I am interested in obtaining a schedule of hikes around Brampton, Mississauga, Toronto, and Caledon. Also, I love to walk but am more of a meanderer. I walk every day for an hour along the Etobicoke Creek, do you think I may be out of my league joining a hiking club? Oh, by the way, I'm 50ish." — *Irene*

"Brampton has its own chapter of the Bruce Trail Club, call 1-800-665-hike to join. You're never too old, Irene, dear." — *HM*

Boot guy did tell me to silicone the boots before I hit the bush, just to make sure. But I don't buy into that. Boots should be ready to wear, not only waterproof but also broken in to prevent foot blisters. Why, just the other day, some boot sales guy told me to wear his boots around the house for a few days in order to break them in before hitting the trail. Hikers, if I can't strap them on and hit the bush immediately, with dry, comfy, pain-free feet at the end of the hike, I don't want to wear the boot.

If you'd like home delivery of a catalogue, call Dunham Boots at 1-800-the-boot or contact Clarence Rosevear at 1-519-756-0002 or Clarence.Rosevear@newbalance.com.

3 *Yo, Fledglings! Tips for New Hikers*

Welcome, beginners. Are you new to hiking? Just starting out this season? Strapping on the boots for the first time? Well, you're gonna have a ball! People hike for a multitude of reasons. For some, it's a low-cost, healthy recreational activity. For others, it's a social occasion, a chance to meet people who love the outdoors as much as they do. All hikers are drawn to the beauty of the land and the release of tension that such an experience induces. Hiking can be an antidote to so much of what plagues our 21st-century urban lifestyle.

Where to hike? Begin close to home — more and more urban centres are developing footpaths linking pockets of green. Then look farther afield for conservation areas or provincial parks. As you become addicted, find out about trail clubs in your immediate area. In addition to the Oak Ridges Trail Association, you may want to try other clubs such as the Toronto Hiking and Conservation Club at 416-964-7281, or the Toronto Bruce Trail Club at 416-690-4433.

One joy of hiking is that it doesn't require a lot of money. If you are just beginning, don't spend your hard-earned cash on equipment until you know that you wish to continue. If you decide to purchase hiking gear, remember, the key to happy hiking is to always look after your feet. For easy trails, a good pair of low cuts will do, but for remote areas or strenuous trails hiking boots are necessary. For carrying a backpack or hiking on rough terrain, it's important that boots rise over the ankle for stability. One foot is usually larger than the other, so footwear should be fitted to the larger foot and thicker socks added to the smaller if necessary.

Hike light. Less weight equals more fun. Hiking trails are usually blazed — a white rectangle painted on trees marks the trail, while a double blaze indicates a turn. If you lose your way, return the way you came to find the previous blaze or sign. Carry your cell phone, a radio and some water for any hike over two hours. Even though you're a sturdy beginner, you'll find your lungs will want to explode while going uphill the first few times; your mind has not yet learned how to make the deal with your body. Legs and lungs have got to find some middle ground, so everyone is happy.

A good remedy when running out of uphill breath is to stop, step off the trail, turn around and appreciate the distance you have already climbed. This enjoyment will also buy you some time to catch your breath. Then, as your lungs start to settle down, you may turn around and survey the next stage in your ascent. Set your own pace, for God's sake! Hiking must be a pleasure, not a chore. If you find yourself heating up, slow down or strip off a layer. And here's a little trick that I'll do while heading up a long incline. I'll shut my mouth and breathe only through my nose. This is not only a good way to set up a rhythm that you might even hang a melody onto, but you'll also regulate your mind, your legs and lungs. To top it all off, your olfactory senses will go crazy with the million smells and scents of the forest. You'll turn back into that animal we all knew you were.

Congrats, new hikers! Welcome aboard.

MEGACITY WARM-UP

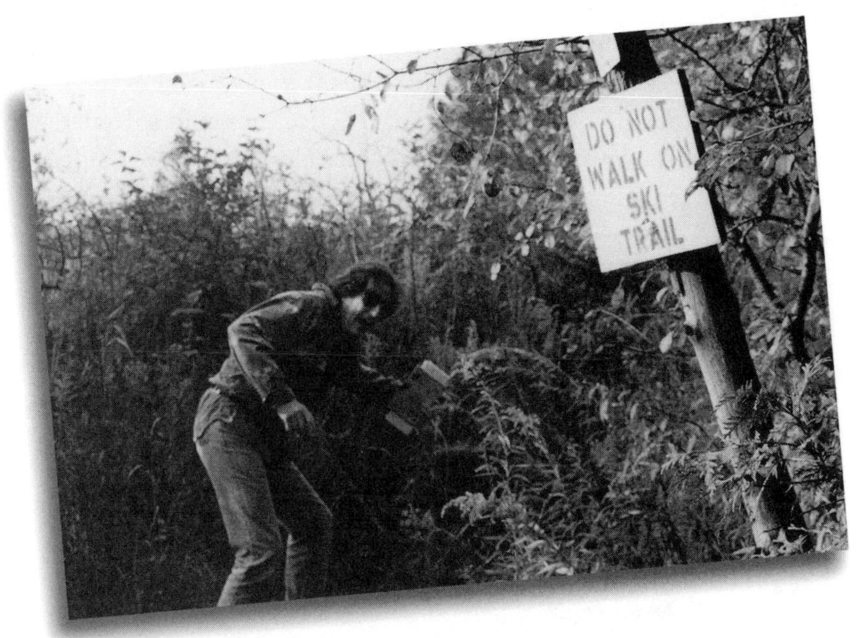

4 Martin Goodman Waterfront Trail

Tracker Dave Bradstreet has just bought a beautiful, roomy, forest-green Range Rover all-terrain vehicle, originally made for some Saudi Arabian sheik who insisted on more leg room in the back than for his chauffeur in the front. We don't use the Range Rover for our hiking expeditions very often because my dog, Rupert, is too stinky to ride in it, but one icy winter day we decided to do a two-car hike of the Toronto waterfront. We met at Ashbridges Bay on the eastern shore of the Beaches, left my car in the parking lot and then drove in Dave's Range Rover west to the old Palais Royale Dance Hall and Sunnyside Beach in Etobicoke, and proceeded to walk the 10 miles back to my car at Ashbridges Bay. What an adventure!

The Martin Goodman Trail started out as icy as a Rosedale matron's glare, but by the time we had put the Argonaut Rowing Club and Marilyn Bell Park behind us, it had started to melt. And once past the CNE and Ontario Place, the cold softened considerably. We stopped at the Second Cup for lattes at Harbourfront, then, upon arrival at Cherry Beach, spring in all her glory had dropped in to say hello. The sun was smiling down on us, and the crocus flowers were seriously considering putting

in an early spring appearance. From -5°C to +9°C in three short hours! We were stripped down to our tee-shirts when we arrived back in Ashbridges, suitably exhausted from our 10-miler, jumped into my car and drove home, tired and happy after living through an excellent hike.

An hour or so later after lunch, back home in the shelter of my Summerhill Hideout, I got a phone call from Tracker Dave. His wonderful wife, Brenda, was wondering where their beautiful Range Rover had gone. It seems in all our spring-weather hiking excitement, we had forgotten to go back to the Palais Royal parking lot to pick up the Sheik's limo. It's at times like this that the immortal words of Rossie Gross's mom, Elsie, always come flooding back to me. Elsie would always say, "Mike, if you can't remember. . . forget it!"

What a weekend, what an adventure, what a life!

5 *Toronto Springtime Hikes: Great March Break Ideas*

By now, you've all received your *Toronto Life* magazine, and inside is a little red booklet called the *Toronto Life Getaway Guide — Wilderness Trips and Great Hiking Trails.* This little booklet is chock full of great weekend hikes for the whole family, such as Crawford Lake Conservation Area at Steeles and the Guelph Line — a hike on the Bruce Trail past an early Iroquois settlement beside Meromictic Lake, complete with Native longhouses true to the era. There's also a 2K trail for wheelchairs. For information, call 905-854-0234.

The *Getaway Guide* also features an inner-city wilderness trail through the Rouge River Valley, the largest urban wilderness park in North America. The 10K trail goes through the Glen Rouge Campgrounds to the Zoo along the river-valley plain and up the high valley walls to the Orchard, Ridge and Vista Trails. The Oak Ridges Moraine in the Durham Regional Forest is also featured, with seven interconnected loop trails providing wide pathways of varying length for easy day hiking. Call 905-723-0023.

But the hike that pushes all of my outdoor adventure buttons is the Haliburton Forest and Wildlife Reserve, where you get to traverse the treetops on a swaying plank suspension bridge no wider than your foot. The world's longest canopy walkway takes nearly two hours to manoeuvre in safety gear used for mountain climbing. The 60,000 acres of Haliburton Forest also include a guided voyageur canoe trip and scenic riverside hikes.

Remember those long days last year with the kids telling you how they're really bored, and isn't there some adventure that Mom and Dad could think up for them to do? Well, now you know. Hiker Mike and *Toronto Life* just gave you some ideas.

Pen Pal: Nancy Gomes

"On your recent radio program, you made mention of a hike where a group of hikers meet every Sunday at 10 AM in a parking lot before heading off together, membership fee is $15. What parking lot was that exactly, and in what area does this hike take place? Would you consider this a hike for beginners, or for the more advanced hiker? Thanks, Hiker Mike!"

— *Nancy Gomes, Mississauga*

"The corner of which I spoke was that of Yonge and York Mills, northwest quadrant. This is the Toronto Hiking and Conservation Club."

— *HM*

6 *Toronto Hiking and Conservation Club*

As I was driving home past the Summerhill Subway stop, I happened upon the biggest group of hikers I have ever seen in one place, all milling about like horses waiting impatiently for the gate to open and start the race. There must have been over 100 hikers, all decked out in their bright, colourful Gore-Tex shells and MEC backpacks, chatting in an animated fashion. So I rolled down the window and shouted "Hello" into

the group, at which time several fellows came over to the car to answer my questions.

They were indeed hikers on their way down into the Don Valley, which they do every Wednesday and Sunday at 10 AM. The name of the group is the Toronto Hiking and Conservation Club, formed in the early 1950s to protect the Don Valley. And every year since, the Toronto hikers, with a membership of 125, have organized programs for Sunday hikes in the countryside surrounding Toronto.

Hikes leave at 10 AM. Hikers dress in sturdy waterproof boots, bring their lunch and a beverage. They realize that they come at their own risk, and the club cannot be held responsible for any mishaps. Visitors are welcome to attend one hike as guests of the club, after which they should apply for membership, which costs $15 for a single and $20 for a family. Call Mira Sadler, the membership secretary, for more info, at 416-489-1983. Some of the hikes the club will be taking are Long Sault, Limehouse Bruce Trail, Guildwood, out Scarborough way, and the mighty Ganaraska Forest Trail.

It was grand to see the hundred hikers ready to set off on the Don Valley Trail. Three cheers for the Toronto Hiking and Conservation Club.

7 *North Humber: Steeles to the 401*

I've just added a new stretch of the Humber River to my Secret Map of All Hikes, from the North Humber Park on Steeles Avenue 'twixt Kipling and Islington all the way downriver past Finch and Albion Road to Pine Point Park, just north of the 401. The pathway is 10 feet wide, paved with asphalt, and is perfect for kids and seniors, families and wheelchairs.

There is only one little problem. You've got to either take the TTC to the Steeles Bridge over the Humber, or your closest relative has got to drop you off by car, 'cuz there is absolutely no parking on Steeles. You'll find that the trail heading south on the west side of the Humber starts out as flat gravel, but quickly

crosses the river to the paved trail just past a 200-year-old mini forest of balsam and spruce tucked up under the big apartments just east of Kipling. This section of the Humber is clean and shallow and smells great, and hearkens back to the Humber's heyday 400 years ago, when it was used as the Great Carrying Place Portage Route to Georgian Bay.

Humber is home to billions of ducks, geese and songbirds, who serenade hikers south past Finch and Islington, under the bridge where the path stretches out along the river for miles to Albion Road. The Humber floodplain has been re-planted with maples, beeches, firs and pines, anchoring the valley soil. The morning sun acts as my poor-man's coat, warming my bones while I hike south past the pretty Etobicoke backyards that bump up against the river.

If you've got the time, and I mean a good two hours, you can walk from Steeles along the Humber to Pine Point Park just north of the 401 (east of Islington off Allenby), and grab the TTC home, or make a day of it and head on down to Lake Ontario, which I reckon should take you five to six hours. Please remember that this Humber trail is an asphalt pathway, so you'll need your cushy, bouncy walking shoes, or you'll end up with sore ankles, knees and hips.

8 *Leslie Street Spitting: Misadventures in Live Radio*

Doncha just love live radio? I know of no other area of show biz that can hurtle you into the Now more violently than live radio. And I used to think a play's opening night in the theatre was heart-stopping! I'm still vibrating physically and emotionally from my experience last Saturday morning.

As most of you who listen to the Big Radio Station know, I phone in to my pal John Donabie, the wacky and wonderful weekend morning host, and let the folks in "radio land" know where to hike, what you'll see along the way, and how to get to and from the trailhead. The 8:20 AM procedure is quite simple: I listen to my little portable radio wherever I may be in the

Megacity, and just as Johnny says, "We'll be talking to Hiker Mike in one minute," I pull out my trusty cell phone and dial the secret number that gains me access to Master Control in the guts of CFRB, where producer Mark Wigmore answers and connects me with John, and *poof*, I'm on the air!

And so it was supposed to go last Saturday. The 8 AM news came and went, I got my cue from John to phone in, I dialed the number and got . . . a busy signal! I tried again, thinking that perhaps someone else doing an interview might be on the line. Once again I got a busy signal.

Now you must picture this. My dog, Rupert the Malamute, and I are standing on a piece of land out in Lake Ontario between the Leslie Street Spit and the Outer Harbour Marina, my little radio in my ear, my report and cell phone in hand, dialing again and again, and being rewarded with a busy signal. John mentions on the air that since I'm not calling him, he's going to call my cell phone, so I stop my now-frantic dialing and await his call, while he goes to more commercials and tries to find me. Nothing happens. No phone call from the station.

It begins to dawn on me that I must be in a non-cellular kind of area, and I start to run for the car about 5 minutes away. Maybe I can find a pay phone or a more cellular-friendly area on the way. And as I'm speeding up Leslie Street out of the industrial waterfront area, I hear John on the air telling everybody that he's reached my answering service.

I am now truly starting to panic. I've let the side down and program boss Steve Kowch and Donabie are going to lynch me next time I'm in the station. By this time I am speeding up Leslie Street, driving with one hand and dialing the station frantically with the other, when suddenly ahead of me the Loblaws Superstore across the Lakeshore looms into view. I charge through the yellow light, wheel into the parking lot and pull up next to the store and park illegally in a disabled persons' spot. I dive into the store's bank of pay phones, whip in a quarter and get John on the other end, who most graciously forgives me and laughs off what must have been for him the longest 10 minutes of totally desperate improvisational radio in his career. He had taken to asking listeners to phone in and suggest good places to go for Sunday brunch.

Pen Pal: Kevin

"Dear Mike: I am an amateur photographer and am still in school. I was wondering if you knew of any nice, scenic hikes where I can take some winter landscape shots and get a little workout? I'm willing to travel about two hours." — *Kevin, Toronto, Ontario*

"Why travel two hours, Kevin? It's all right here in the Metro Conservation Areas: Kortright and Albion Hills, 30 minutes north of Toronto; Rouge River and Claremont, 35 minutes east of Toronto; Glen Eden–Kelso and Hilton Falls, 40 minutes west of Toronto; and Toronto Islands and the Martin Goodman Trail, 10 minutes south to the lake. Call the Metro Conservation Authority for directions, at 416-661-6600." — *HM*

Now that would be pretty much enough stress and strain for anyone on a quiet Saturday morning, but when Hiker Mike messes up, it's rarely done in small measure. I got back to the illegal parking spot and found a bright-yellow parking ticket for $50 on my windshield. Then I realized that I had left my trusty dog, Rupert, back at the hike on the lake, so the panic started to rise again, phoenix-like, from the warm ashes of my lower guts, and off I sped to find my dog. Thankfully, I did, only to discover

that I had left my prescription glacier sunglasses back at Loblaws on top of the pay phone, along with my portable radio, hiking report and cell phone.

And so it went. By the time I got home, I had succeeded in disappearing up my own backside: I was well and truly freaked out, ready to crawl back into bed and spend the weekend. And it was only 10 AM Saturday morning. Doncha just love live radio?

9 *Hit the Trail, Jack! Get Outta the Megacity and Hike*

North • Get outta the Megacity and head up north of Highway 7 and Major Mackenzie, up into the Oak Ridges Moraine around Aurora–Richmond Hill–Lake Wilcox–St. Georges. The Caledons are very colourful in the early fall up the Airport Road to Glen Haffy Park at Highway 9, and Terra Cotta, land of the red earth, up Winston Churchill Boulevard. But the emerald in the Caledon crown is Belfountain and the Forks of the Credit River. Lots of Toronto folks drive up Highway 10, north of Brampton, and spend the day walking the trails or antiquing.

West • Out Halton Hills way, north of Milton, is the Niagara Escarpment. That's apple country. Most folks go to Chudleighs, but it gets pretty crowded, so keep going north along Highway 25 to the 10th Sideroad. Turn right and follow the signs to Williams Apple Farm on the 4th Line, north of the 10 Sideroad. Sandy and Eldon Williams are old friends, and you can pick your own goldens, empires, mutsus, and more.

East • Closer to town, north of the 401 between Meadowvale and Morningside, runs the Rouge River Valley from Steeles down to Lake Ontario. Go to the Zoo entrance or Pearce House, park your car, and hike the Vista Trail along the ridge, high above the Rouge.

I understand that there's a great ravine buried in the wilds of Scarborough that's as good a hike as Algonquin Park. It's

called the Birkdale Ravine, and it runs south off Lawrence just east of Ellesmere.

If you're new to this hiking thing, here's what you do. Head off into the hills — the Haltons, the Caledons, or the Albions — until you hit a dirt road. Keep driving until you can pull off and park, next to a bridge over a creek. Maybe there's a path heading upriver, or maybe a road allowance continuing on past a dead-end road. Just follow your nose and take the adventure. What's the worst that can happen to you? Someone will yell at you to get the hell off their private property! Just apologize profusely and head back from whence you came. Like they say in Tangiers, "Stay on the main road," but never forget the immortal words of N.Y. Yankees catcher Yogi Berra: "When you come to the fork in the road, take it!"

Pen Pal: Hefty Heidi from Hamilton

"Hi. My family and I recently hiked part of the Bruce Trail leading to Tew's Falls overlooking Dundas Ontario. It was just enough of a hike for a heavy woman, sedentary man and two 10-year-olds! We were wondering whether there is another trail that runs along the valley to the base of Tew's Falls rather than along the ridge above. Thanks."

— Heidi, Hamilton, Ontario

"Hi, Heidi: You can walk by trail to the base of Tew's Falls. Grant Leigh of the Bruce Trail Club says there is a great book you should buy called Waterfalls of the Niagara Escarpment. It gives you all the maps and trails you'll need: Webster's Falls, Tew's Falls, Hilton and Ball's Falls."

— HM

"Thanks a lot, Hiker Mike! Last week we started at Webster's Falls, went down the stairs into the gorge and hiked along the path, with the river to our left. It was like another world in that gorge, and the further away from the falls the less populated the trail became. We did notice that not much wildlife comes out during the day — we spotted just one downy woodpecker. Happy Hiking!"

— Heidi

I'd been out that way only once before. Hamilton was just beyond my normal Sunday-morning distance, so I'd found myself at Borer's Falls and the Rock Chapel Sanctuary only with an effort and extra time on my hands. But, boy, was that Dundas–Waterdown hike a pleasure, which I tried to pass on to you in the first Hiker Mike book.

So, putting aside a whole day and rousing my Sherpa pals Bradstreet and Sorensen at an inordinately early time on a Sunday morning, we three headed out the Queen Elizabeth Way west toward Hamilton's Highway 403, and when we came upon the scenic old Highway 8 to Galt–Cambridge, we started our car climb up the mountain and past the sleepy little town of Dundas. At the top of the big hill, we continued up Brock Road, while Highway 8 shot off to the left toward Galt. Heading further north on Brock, we then turned right on Harvest Road and right again on Short Road and followed the signs to the Spencer Gorge Park at the top of Tew's Falls.

Tew's Falls, at 135 feet, is almost as high as Niagara's Horseshoe Falls, and is shaped like a giant limestone bowl. If you follow the beautiful, wide and well-used trail along the high mountain ridge to the south, the white blazes of the Bruce Trail will deliver you up to Dundas Peak, where all will be made clear: a most spectacular view of the Dundas Valley, with Hamilton Harbour, Stoney Creek in the distance, Dundas and Ancaster directly below, and Hamilton Mountain heading south, all the way to St. Catharine's.

After absorbing as much vista as our minds could bear, we headed down the white trail to the base of the mountain and the railroad tracks some 200 feet below, by means of two giant traverses, switching back across the mountainside flanks. Following the white trail west, almost to the bridge over Highway 8, we noticed both the white and blue blazes of the Bruce heading north into the bush and a sign announcing the trail to the old Dundas Station, a short cut forming a 6.3K loop back to Tew's Falls on the blue trail, or the longer pathway riverside to Webster's Falls along the white trail, which we chose. The pathway climbed a series of railroad ties into the big oak forest. We met an entire wolf-cub pack, some seniors in great shape who hike this loop daily, security-minded women hikers in tag teams, and loads of well-to-do European men named Karl, with dogs. Don't ask me why.

Ron and Sue Riley, in their late 60s, have been coming here to hike for over 50 years. Norman and Ruth Best left Toronto to make their home high up on the mountain. Even Rupert, my then 12-year-old malamute Wonder Dog, had little problem navigating these trails, including the 200-odd metal stairs leading up the side of Webster's Falls. Rupie even stopped for a lie-down, swim and drink in the shallows at the base of the Falls, while the rest of us watched and took pictures as the Flamborough Fire Department belayed and rappelled up and down the 100 feet of the Falls, as sightseeing hiking families cheered on the brave firemen.

The park above Webster's Falls is beautifully maintained and manicured, with grass and gravel walkways over arching stone bridges, and well-marked signs to keep you on the trail back to Tew's Falls in the Spencer Gorge and your car.

The loop takes three hours and any way you cut it, the Dundas Mountain loop is the best that hiking gets, and once done,

Pen Pal: Seymour Applebaum

"There are plenty of good hikes in the Niagara Region, some even have waterfalls. Try Niagara Glen, just off the Niagara Parkway. It's a great hike to experience getting close to the Niagara River. The trailhead is just across from the Niagara Falls Whirlpool Golf Course. You start off by descending a metal staircase, then you're into a challenging hike. There's a map of the trails in the park just before you head toward the staircase. The trail is very well marked. We took our dog Macie along. Dogs don't like metal staircases, but she managed to make it anyway, with lots of encouragement from other hikers."

— *Seymour Applebaum, Oak Ridges, Ontario*

"Seymour also first alerted me to the Oak Ridges Trail in Aurora years ago. Good on you, Seymour, you intrepid explorer, you." — *HM* you'll go back countless times for more. Just like one of the European dog-walkers named Karl, who hikes the loop twice a day and has for 18 years, says, "The Spencer Gorge Wilderness Area is like good salmon steak. You just can't get enough!"

12 *Bruce Trail Membership*

You've heard me speak many times about one of our Canadian National Treasures — the Niagara Escarpment — a mammoth limestone ridge running from Niagara Falls and Queenston in the south all the way up through St. Catharines, Hamilton, and past the 401 at Milton — the better part of 420 miles to Collingwood, Wiarton and Tobermory in the north.

This 200-to-300-foot outcropping is so unique in its fauna and flora that the United Nations has designated the Niagara Escarpment its own World Biosphere Reserve, along with Florida's Everglades and South America's Galapagos Islands. And running along the top of this world wonder is our very own Bruce Trail, winner of this year's Golden Boot Award for Best Damned Hiking Trail in the Megacity.

I have made mention recently of the Toronto Bruce Trail's membership phone number, 1-800-665-hike, for all of you outdoor people who were thinking of joining. So it was quite serendipitous that I should receive my Bruce Trail quarterly magazine, called *Footnotes*, this past week.

I always look forward to getting *Footnotes* as part of my $40 membership, because the 34-page almanac is a hiking subculture unto itself. It contains wonderful in-depth articles on upcoming weekend hikes; how to keep your feet happy when buying new boots and socks; when, where and how to go about becoming a hike leader; and outdoor weekend courses on map and compass reading.

Any information you beginner hikers need in order to become a Bruce Trail Club member can be found on the net by typing in www.torontobrucetrailclub.org. There's no better place to start.

13 A Beginner Hike to Backpacker's Bench

Tracker Dave Bradstreet and I were out snooping around a little-known section of the Bruce Trail last weekend. We had found the trail at the corner of the Coolihan Sideroad and Glen Haffy Road, up where Highway 50 meets Highway 9. Lots of cars parked around the trailhead, though we passed only two runners on our way to a most spectacular high-ground vista in the Caledon Hills.

About 30 minutes from our car, we climbed up out of a dark-green cedar river valley onto a high deciduous plain. But the trail just kept heading up to a grassy crest, on top of which sat a wide and low wooden backpacker's bench looking out over what I can truly say is one of the most majestic panoramas of the Caledon and Albion Hills.

Trailmate Pen Pals: Jennifer and Dave

"Great meeting the Hiking Guru himself on Saturday. What a coincidence. Of all the trails in all the countries of the world . . . Thought we'd drop you a line to let you know that we did it! We completed the 20K Hilton Falls loop. Not in record time by any means — it was starting to get dark and we were getting a little nervous wondering if we were going to have to spend the night in the woods with the other wildlife. As I stumbled out onto the road, Dave told me I looked like some of the people crossing the finish line of the triathlon in Sydney. That last hour or so was pretty tough — but definitely worth it. It was our best hike to date. The wooded trails are my favourite. Happy Hiking!" —*Jennifer and Dave*

Although the wind was screaming furiously all around us, we were sheltered on the bench by great, fat, old-growth maple and pine. Once we were rested, we found the bench difficult to leave. The wind was pure and cool and clean, while the vista to the north and east formed a great green coniferous carpet rolling out towards the misty horizon. Reminded me strongly of the Great Smoky Mountains of North Carolina, where I walked as a boy. I am recommending this as a good beginner hike — one hour to the bench and back.

Directions: Take Highway 50 north to Highway 9 west to Glen Haffy Road south to Coolihans Sideroad, or head up Airport Road, and right on Coolihans. Park your car and hike the half hour along Mother Nature's most beautiful Bruce, up to Backpacker's Bench.

14 *Ring Around the Quarry*

When we moved back to Big Smoke, I promised my Bruce Trail neighbours never to divulge the location of our former Hiker Hideout to anyone, because our little community of friends and cottages thrives at the end of a dirt road leading into thousands of hectares of high-country forest atop the Niagara Escarpment somewhere north of Milton. So in order to keep that promise, I will show you another way to access perhaps the most ruggedly wonderful hiking trail this side of Tobermory.

Over the past 20 years, I have become increasingly familiar with this mammoth quadrant filled with rivers, lakes and limestone quarries, and have watched as the Bruce Trail Toronto Club made its inroads, clearing the trail and moving carefully around the natural features with both the white-blazed Main Trail, and most recently the 21K of the blue-blazed Hilton Falls Side Trail, forming a giant loop circumscribing one of the biggest limestone and gravel quarries in Southern Ontario.

If you've ever driven up the Sea to Sky Highway running north through the Coast Mountains from Vancouver towards Whistler's ski heaven, you'll recall the rush you felt seeing the mile-high stone wall of Squamish's "The Chief" for the first time. That's somewhat the same feeling you'll get while driving the 401 west and coming upon the high green ridges of the Niagara Escarpment's leaping giant, the Milton Outlier, with her chalky white canyons diving dramatically into the Nasagawaya Canyon — a truly wondrous outdoor paradise. And if you were

to exit the 401 at Highway 25 north and then turn west on the Campbellville 5 Sideroad, you would drive past the Greystone Golf Club, nestled up snug under the mountain, before arriving at the Halton 6th Line. And if you were to turn north to the top of the hill, you would see the Halton Golf Club on your left and the stone cave opening to the Bruce Trail on your right, with plenty of parking on the wide right-hand shoulder.

The Bruce then takes you east and north through the forest along the high ridge that lets you see Lake Ontario from Burlington, Oakville and Mississauga, all the way across the ancient seabed to the skyline of Toronto's bank buildings, the Skydome and the CN Tower (from 40 miles away!). But mind your feet, because the path is quite dangerous — full of loose and large, rocky limestone-boulder outcroppings. So it's best to hike carefully, between lookout and rest stops, keeping an eye on your next footfall. Many high lookouts range along the ridge where the hiker can kick up, have a Coke and see it all — to my mind, the most spectacular section of the Bruce Trail in Southern Ontario.

The trail of white blazes spills you out onto a red-'n'-rusty steel sky bridge crossing over the Dufferin Aggregates Road, where parades of giant dump trucks full of gravel pass dustily underneath.

It's about an hour's walk, northeast along the ridge, to the Hilton Falls Side Trail's blue blazes, steering you west into the heavy, hilly bush that'll take you across the town line, past the Willowbrook Bed and Breakfast at the bottom of the hill. The pathway then crashes back into the forest for a happy jaunt on an easy trail that nudges you out over Sixteen Mile Creek and onto the sleepy 6th Line, where you'll turn left and head south for a half hour's soft shuffle back down to your car. Count on a good three hours of rough-and-tumble hiking on this Bruce Trail circuit.

One of my little pleasures is to sit in the shade on the stony edge of the golf course and watch the duffers blow their putts, while acting as a gallery of one, with polite applause when one of them actually finds the hole, before jumping into my chariot

and heading home. Remember to leave your car windows open a crack before the hike so you don't fry your butt upon re-entry.

The Bruce Trail Ring Around the Quarry–Hilton Falls Side Trail loop is a good and strenuous adventure, so take your sturdy rock-friendly boots, your hat and bug spray and plenty of H_2O and maybe even a pair of binoculars for the eyeball's smorgasbord that awaits your viewing pleasure.

Pen Pals Mike and Susan: A Warning

"Hi! We really enjoy listening to your hiking reports on the weekends. Perhaps you could warn your listeners not to leave their wallets or purses in the car while they are hiking. A few weeks ago, I locked my purse in the trunk and when I got back to the car an hour and a half later, someone had smashed in the back window of our hatchback and taken my purse. My husband and I have been camping, canoeing and hiking together for almost 30 years and we have never had a problem before. From now on, I will take only what I need and carry it in a waist pouch."

— *Mike and Susan, Queensville, Ontario*

"I'm so sorry for your misfortune. This is the first I've heard of this kind of burglary. I will be most careful from now on and put the warning on the show." — *HM*

15 *Williams Apple Orchard*

Last Sunday, Bradstreet and I went out hiking and put in a good three hours of fairly rugged booting through the rocky limestone outcroppings that dot the trail along the top of the world-famous Niagara Escarpment. Tracker Dave did a fancy shoulder roll to save a broken ankle early on in the hike but sprained it just the same, and my back quietly slipped out of safe harbour some hours later. But what we two walking wounded did manage to do between the end of the hike and the hospital beds back in town was to drop into Williams Apple

Orchard to see our old friends Sandy and Eldon and pick up our fall load of Ida reds and golden delicious, along with gallons of their apple cider.

I've known the Williams since they pulled up Toronto stakes and moved to green acres. This year was the best crop ever — all that rain and sunshine of the past summer — producing the fattest and most juicy apples in the Williams's 10-year history, until the farm was visited by that freak hailstorm that devastated 60 to 70 percent of their crop.

Now you might ask what a hailstorm does to an orchard. Apart from knocking the plump, ripening fruit out of the trees, the hail also bombards the apples like comets and asteroids hitting the earth, and though the pock-marked fruit is still good and fit to eat, the apples on those trees tend to look like a bleacher full of acne-riddled teenagers at a high-school pep rally.

The Williams farm always gives you the opportunity to pick your own bushel of beautiful apples for less than half of what you'd pay anywhere else, so you can take the kids and eat your way through a weekend afternoon while getting your exercise hiking in their beautiful orchard.

Head out the 401 west to 25 north. Turn right on the 10th Sideroad and left on the 4th Line north. Williams Apple Orchards are right behind Andrews Scenic Acres. Say "Hi" to Sandy and Eldon from Hiker Mike. They're both as sweet as their apples.

16 *Nasagawaya Canyon*

Nasa-ga-waya! Say it like an Ojibwa. *Mnnn! Na-sa-ga-way-ya!* That's exactly what it means. Really big, exceedingly deep valley with sheer, steep walls on both sides.

If you've ever had the singular pleasure of leaving the city of Vancouver and heading away from Horseshoe Bay up the Sea to Sky Highway 99 towards Squamish, you know the joy of winding your way through B.C.'s Coast Mountains until you round that one last curve, which leaves you gawking in astonishment at the mile-high mountain of rock wall called The Chief — every rock climber's wet dream. You can stand for hours gazing at the cracks and ruts and crevasses of this massive vertical, while planning your imaginary ascent and wondering why B.C. has all the great Canadian climbing walls.

Well, grouse no longer, Bubba. Pay a visit to Southern Ontario's largest limestone climbing wall, Rattlesnake Point. Rattlesnake Point stands on the extreme south end of the Milton Outlier, a stand-alone mesa rising out of an ancient limestone sea that has been carved away from the main ridge of our own Niagara Escarpment by two rivers, the Bronte and the Sixteen Mile Creek, 30 miles south and west of Toronto in the sleepy little town of Milton. You can see the Outlier approaching on the 401 coming from the Megacity. Glen Eden–Kelso Ski Club runs up her wide and furry green flanks, and at her feet to the west a very deep and wide pre-glacial forest canyon called Nasagawaya. The mighty Bruce Trail gives us a front-row seat to the whole show.

This past week the Urban Sherpas found their way to Derry Road and Twiss Road North, one concession west of the Guelph Line, where the bright white blazes of the Bruce Trail headed east into the high deciduous forest towards Crawford Lake Conservation Area and the mighty Nasagawaya Canyon. Crawford Lake is great for cross-country skiing as well — the trails are gourmet, wide and welcoming, complete with memorial resting benches dedicated to dearly departed hikers like John Earl Thomas. The trail leads directly to the lookout at Canyon Ridge, then over we jump, down the steep walls to the canyon floor.

Now begins a cardiovascular clinic, heading straight up the Jack Leitch Side Trail, as you start climbing to the top of the Eastern Ridge, hundreds of feet above the canyon's floor. Hikers, you owe it to yourself to check out your heart and lungs on the walls of the Nasagawaya.

The hike is three hours from Twiss Road, north of Derry to Rattlesnake Point. Do what we did and park one car on Twiss and the other car at Rattlesnake parking lot on top of the Appleby Line, and hike your butt off. Rattlesnake may not be as steep as The Chief out in Squamish, B.C., but the Nasagawaya walls will pump your blood. Say Nasagawaya properly and your chest bone should vibrate. Nasagawaya! I have spoken!

17 *Twelve-Step Tenting*

I'm not much of a tent guy anymore. The thought of crawling into a mummy-shaped sleeping bag and rolling around on the rocky ground all night by myself does nothing for me. That's not to say I didn't love it when I was a kid. I used to make tents under the dining room table with old Mennonite quilts from the trunk, and when I was 12 I moved into a backyard tent for the summer. The orange plastic ground sheet sewn into the floor of that tent killed our backyard grass real good.

The first time I went up to Everest Base Camp, I shared a two-man tent with Canadian Himalayan guide Joe Pilaar. Joe was a great tentmate except when he slept, he'd stop breathing. Sleep apnea happens sometimes around 20,000 feet. Scared the hell out of me. First you'd hear a snore from Joe, then absolutely nothing for two minutes. I spent the below-zero night trying to sleep on the icy, rocky glacier and waking Joe up every 15 minutes — the longest, coldest night of my life. At one point I crawled out of the tent and into the teeth of a 30-knot blow so I could have a pee. As I stood there shaking with cold, I bent over to pull up my long johns and proceeded to puke and poop simultaneously; dysentery and altitude sickness can team up to cause some unforgettable moments at the top of the world. I blame a good deal of this on tenting. So now I like to hike 20 miles a day and spend the evenings at a good B&B or hotel with a sauna and hot tub and an excellent restaurant.

This little vignette about total loss of control while trekking is a cheap and sassy way of getting around to telling you that Ed has opened Tent Town for the summer season. If you've ever driven up Mississauga Road, north of the 401 but south of Steeles, you will have seen the big pasture field on the left, chock full of over 100 tents of every size, from the teeny-tiny two-man tents up to the plantation version with the screened-in sunporches, four bedrooms and a card-playing area complete with wet bar.

Tent Town is owned and operated by Tent Man Ed, a colourful old character who just happens to be a good friend of my old friends Bill W. and Dr. Bob. Some of you know them too.

Ed goes around to the Sportsmen's Show and buys up all the floor-stock tents for next to nothing, brings them back and sets them up in Tent Town. Ed will either sell these high-end, top-of-the-line tents to you for a lot less than retail, or Tent Man Ed will rent you the tent of your choice, along with all the camping gear you need — sleeping bags, air mattresses, Coleman stoves, cookware, lanterns, canopies and tarps — the whole kit, so you don't have to lay out a grand or two in order to go to the Rouge Campgrounds for the weekend.

Ed tells me that Ted Woloshyn rents his tents there when he and Mayor Hazel throw those big Mississauga celebrity functions and golf tourneys. I've never heard tell of a place other than Tent Town where you can rent all your camping gear, so give the Tent Man a call. Ed's number is 905-813-8003, or head out the 401 and north on Mississauga Road. There's a big red-and-white sign out front that says, "Tent Town, Sorry, We're Open."

18 *My Secret Love*

Been feeling kind of deep-winter gnarly lately. I start to get down on people and situations. Don't feel much like writing or socializing. Can't even work up the energy for a Sunday morning "Chapel in the Pines" hike. Got to guilt myself into going by quietly muttering stuff like, "How can you live with yourself, you lazy loafer?" or "What are you going to talk about on the radio next weekend?"

And so I'm very grateful for my built-in auto-pilot cruise control that self-activates on those bleary February mornings and moves me bodily towards the trailhead, no matter how much my sleepy head tries to persuade me otherwise. And of course once I hit the trail all the half-empty-glass thoughts and feelings disappear, and I turn into that 12-year-old horny hiking fool again. And so today, I'd like to let it all hang out and compose a Valentine's card to the passion and love of my life: hiking. How do I love thee? Let me count the ways!

Moving out of downtown Toronto, coffee in hand, searching the Southern Ontario geography for a potential trailhead always kickstarts my sense of adventure. Today I'm not the only slow-moving car on the Escarpment Sideroad looking for a trail leading into the forest. Hiking is a fast-growing sport, and lord knows there's still plenty of room on the trail for all of us. The Nature-in-all-her-splendour movie is happily playing on my windshield screen. I spot the Bruce Trail's fat white blazes, pull safely off the gravel road and park. I crawl out, lock the beast and breathe in a major hit of pure forest oxygen. Jumping into the bush, my feet land firmly on a trail that is frozen hard and grittily granular, which makes for great traction. Rupert and I move quickly along the top of the snow, travelling lightly and keeping time to the rhythmic pealing of the Campbellville United Church bell, calling us all to the Sunday morning Worship in the Woods.

We're running through the forest now, next to the Sixteen Mile Creek, the sun wildly bouncing off the rapids and throwing snow shadows into the bush. On the first big toboggan slide downhill, my boots dig in and hold, bringing me safely to the valley floor, which I cross quietly and quickly and then charge pell-mell uphill to the high ridge trail above. Rupert hits the top first and is swooning happily over an immense pile of black-bear poop, his eyes glazed over as he whiffs deeply. Time stands still for Rupert the Malamute; he almost faints from primal fecal pleasure. I soon find myself standing on a new Bruce Trail bridge over the torrent, in the centre of a deep, warm, February sun pocket. My imagination runs away with me, and my head starts tossing future hopes and dreams, like gold and silver coins, into the swiftly moving rapids.

By this time, about an hour into the journey, I am at peace. All the stress and strain and tension has left my body, and the endorphins have clicked in, reinstating my feeling of well-being and putting my sorry mind at ease. Invariably I find that hiking brings me back to earth. If I take a heavy problem with me out there on the trail, most times I return home with a viable solution for that problem.

Spirit, mind and body — the YMCA way of life. It's tough to put all three together in the midst of a cold, dark Canadian winter, but that's exactly what hiking does for me. I always come home from a hike grateful to be alive, with friends and family who love me and whom I love in return. Hiking gives me that. The greatest compliment came from my daughter Katy Brando on returning from a Bruce Trail hike. "Daddy," she said, "you smell just like Temagami."

Pen Pal: Rolling Margaret

"Dear Hiker Mike: I am an avid hiker. I should say I was an avid hiker, until I messed up both my hamstrings three years ago. Now you might say I am hamstrung when it comes to hitting the trail. I have a short walking duration, little tolerance for hills, and have not hiked since the last time I tried and darn near died in the trees along the trail. My hamstrings completely pooped out on me and I had to crawl back to my car. Hiker Mikey, do you know of any trails that are wheelchair accessible? I can walk short distances and need to rest frequently. I long to get out once in a while but don't really know how or where." — *Margaret, Halton Hills*

"All river valley and waterfront trails in the Megacity are wheelchair friendly. Don, Rouge, Humber along the Martin Goodman Trail and Leslie Street Spit on Lake Ontario. Call 416-661-6600, Toronto Conservation Authority, and they'll send you a brochure." — *HM*

19 *Rockwood Hike into History*

This past week I took a grand riverside hike back to my boyhood along the Eramosa River in the pretty little village of Rockwood.

I lived in Rockwood, over the top of the Red & White grocery store — Jack Kirby & Sons — when I was 14 years old. I spent countless hours exploring the ancient limestone seabed to the west of Rockwood, towards Eden Mills and Guelph, where giant sphinx-like stone monoliths rise solemnly out of the shallow river, sheltering deep kettle lakes and potholes riddled with cedar and pine. But I could never find the path across Highway

Pen Pal: A Letter from Jane of Eden Mills

"Hello, Mike, Greetings from Country Spirit B&B in Eden Mills. In answer to your queries about hiking in our area..."

Hike Number 1 • As mentioned to you by phone, there is an old trail to an abandoned limestone quarry, between Rockwood and Everton along the Eramosa River. From Highway 7 it runs east of the river, and as there is not a good access to it, one must find one's own. Turning right at the Stonebarn Estates, when on Highway 7 going from Acton to Rockwood, one can find there are paths between the houses to get on it. As there is an old law that demands the public right of way, one could start, keeping close to the river, right at Highway 7, but some landowners do not like this, and are not familiar with these rights. The trail winds along the river, crossing it at times. We have tried a few times to get through to Everton following the river, without success. The underbrush gets too heavy, and there is private land as well. Just the same, it is a lovely trail to explore for an hour or so, maybe longer, and in early spring on a snowy, sunny March day the activity of the birds there was amazing.

Hike Number 2 • Following Highway 7 to Guelph, turn south on Wellington 29 (past Rockwood and before Guelph) and then left into Eden MIlls. Don't follow the road over the two bridges, but continue straight ahead to a dead end. Opening the fence, you will find the cross-country trail, which can be walked in the fall and spring (summer it is too buggy). It winds in a large loop over the outrunners of the escarpment and offers spectacular views. It can be done in about one hour, and if you start at my house, you can add 10 to 15 minutes to it, one way.

Hike Number 3 • The Eramosa River, which runs behind my house, is in places too shallow for a canoe to pass. The water rises to between the ankle and mid-calf only. And so our latest invention is a "river walk," wonderfully refreshing on a hot summer day. The riverbed is firm, and mainly covered with rocks, the water streams fast and is crystal clear. It is most pleasant walking with old runners or Teva sandals and a walking stick. We do not cover a great distance this way, but at the bridge on the Indian Trail one can venture along both directions. The bugs are not bad over the water, and it is a great way to splash around on a warm summer afternoon. Small crayfish can be seen darting between the stones, as well as an occasional fish, but they prefer deeper water.

Hike Number 4 • At the south end of Eden Mills passes the Speed River Trail, which turns into the Guelph Radial Trail, running from Preston to Limehouse, and is 24.6K long. It follows the Eramosa River to the Blue Springs Creek. A detailed map of this trail can be found in the Guelph Hiking Trail Handbook, which is published by the Guelph Hiking Club. The club has a schedule of guided hikes as well. I found very precise maps of each area made especially for hikers in the following paper, "Focus on Conservation Halton," summer/fall 1998 edition. You could contact them at 905-336-1158. Happy hiking!"

— *Jane Isbrucker, Country Spirit Bed and Breakfast, Eden Mills*

7, leading eastward and north from Rockwood, upriver to the cub camp village of Everton. Instead, I found only thick black cedar, bramble and impassible thickets of marshy bush. Then old FM radio guy Tim Lang let slip the secret entrance to the trailhead, and if you promise not to breathe a word, I'll share his golden secret with you.

Coming from downtown Toronto, you must take the 401 west to Highway 25 north to Acton. You'll bump into Highway 7 west, which will take you through Rockwood past the delightful Saunders Bakery (best sugar donuts in the entire world) to the Rockmosa Community Centre. Park your car, cross the road to Jackson Street and begin your hike. At the end of Jackson Street you'll find an old stone gate. Jump it, follow the wide cinder pathway down to the river and head north, keeping the river on your right. The pathway will try to dead end you in a rocky box-canyon quarry, but double back and stick to the river, heading north, walking upstream, keeping the stone giants guarding your left flank and the languid Eramosa your right. Two hours tops. You'll bump up against a big fence with a wooden wigwam. Go no further. Private property! And the owners have told me personally, so let's honour the request.

This peaceful hike along the Eramosa River is almost a religious experience; truly a sacred hike in my never-ending Quest for the Holy Trail. Speaking of which. . .

20 *Home of Gitchi Manitou*

On a day just like today, almost 400 years ago, an Ojibwa war messenger moves quickly, soundlessly down the foot-wide pathway. He is one of the first true *coureurs de bois*, a runner of the Canadian woods, normally bringing words and messages from the chieftains to the warrior bands protecting the outlying lands of the Credit River Valley, a country so rich in game and lush in scenery that it was given the name "Home of the Great God Gitchi Manitou" by the tribal elders.

Every pit-a-pat footfall of the messenger brings him closer to his meeting on the coast of Lake Ontario, this time with the French white man Etienne Brulé, the brave explorer who has been sent by Samuel de Champlain to find the river passage to Georgian Bay and the bountiful fur and game that lie far beyond the Great Lakes.

The news is not good. The Credit River is not only too shallow for canoe navigation, but also arises from a series of springs not 50 miles from the Lake of Ontario, and so would serve no purpose as a great carrying trail northward. (The Humber River just to the east would soon become just that!) But the bad news delivered to Etienne Brulé this fateful day would prove to be wonderful tidings for hikers and outdoor adventurers from that time onward.

Not 30 kilometres from the downtown centre of Toronto lies the most heavenly, serene and untrammeled river valley imaginable, blessed with a footpath as old as time and as quiet as a forest grave, save for the cries of the hawk and the turkey vulture. The Credit Valley Footpath winds its way along the sparkling shallows and up and down the steep, deep-green walls through fern pastures primeval, from Terra Cotta to Georgetown, past an ancient riverside village fit for a Breughal painting — Glen Williams.

Standing atop the high ridge of Cemetery Hill, overlooking the 200-year-old village, the mill town of Glen Williams nestles itself into a giant horseshoe bend of the Credit. The stone churches and faded red-brick houses are all only semi-visible through the thick, green canopy, climbing up out of the sleepy nook to the cliffs of the magnificent Niagara Escarpment just beyond.

Recently, CBC television featured the Canada 2000 "Assault on Mount Everest" expedition, reporting from the little village of Kumjung just to the north of the Buddhist temple village of Tangboche, situated above 13,000 feet. All trekkers and climbers must pass through Tangboche, a verdant sky saddle spanning two great mountains, deep in the Khumbu region of Nepal, on their way to the Base Camp of Mount Everest. The sight of the giant pine forests and the blooming rhododendron made my heart ache to return to the Himalayas once more, so I did the next best thing — I grabbed my backpack, flung Rupert the Malamute into the back of my wagon and headed out the 401 west to Winston Churchill Boulevard North and parked at the southwest corner of the 22nd Sideroad and the 10th Line, where I picked up the bright-blue blazes of the Credit Valley Footpath Section of the mighty Bruce Trail.

Just like Tangboche Trail, the Credit Valley Footpath is an exceedingly arduous trek up the steep canyons and valley walls and would have run along the river were it not for spring flooding and erosion. The pathway switches back and forth, to and fro, up and down the steep inclines, executing a series of

Pen Pal: Marjorie, of the Cheltenham Badlands

"I heard you talking about Terra Cotta on Sunday and thought you are the perfect person to ask about the area in my picture — Olde Base Line between Winston Churchill and Highway 10. I have been intrigued with this for a long time and did not know exactly what to call it. Is it part of the Moraine or Terra Cotta?" — *Marjorie, Mississauga*

"Dear Marjorie: Welcome to the world-famous Cheltenham Badlands."

— *HM*

heart-stopping, mind-bending suicide verticals for 30 minutes or more before the trail finally evens out along the high ridge, with an amazing 5K view of the great Escarpment looming all smoky through the trees to the south and west.

A word to the doggy people: the fences have been stretched tight to the posts and snugly fit to the ground around the stiles, with no holes for dogs, so leave big Bowser at home for this one unless you still possess the strength to fling him over the top of the fence.

Following the Credit Valley south to Glen Williams, you'll run smack into a magical red-pine forest (my favourite), the most graceful and beautiful of all evergreens, the Botticelli of conifers, shamelessly flaunting the burnt reds, pinks and siennas of their barks. And underfoot, the soft pine-needle carpet beckons, all awash in lush red Renaissance hues and tints (but I digress).

One hour into the journey, you come down to the river-valley plain and cross a clean little spring-fed creek, into which Rupert and I did dare to bend and drink our fill, before meeting up with the noisy and loquacious Credit River. She kept us company as we travelled along the verdant and stately backyards of the lucky Glen Williams residents just across the river. You do have to tightrope a tree trunk across a tributary of the Credit, but it's wide and welcoming and only a couple of

feet above the raging rapids. You'll make it — just bring along a change of socks in case of a soaker. The trail brings you into the back door of Georgetown at River Drive and Maple Avenue — big bridge and old mill. The footpath is part of a 16K link trail stretching from Terra Cotta down to Highway 7 at Norval. Definitely advanced *coureurs de bois* or hard-nosed Gramma. And just like the Everest Base Camp hike, the degree of difficulty of this three-hour hike is matched only by its beauty.

It was the great Sherpa mountain climber Tenzing Norgay who once said, "Dance with Chomo Lungma and she'll clasp you to her mountainous bosoms." And it's Hiker Mike who always says, "Hop up off your transcendental butts and hit the Comeback Trail to Fitness."

Pen Pal: Robert, on the Grand River's Elora Gorge

"Hi, Mike: I am John Donabie's friend. You left a great message on my voice mail giving advice on hikes in the Beamsville area. I didn't go... I went to the Elora Gorge instead. I have never been on a hike before (I usually do other types of exercise) ... it was a glorious experience to feel nature's silence in the air, with the gently flowing Grand River as the backdrop. I loved walking up and down the paths and into the Gorge. I loved the scenery ... we hiked for hours and hours. It was wonderful. I can hardly wait until the next hike. Thanks again." — *Robert Lindsay, Milne*

"Elora's a 200-year-old mill town, built with stone, along the Grand River. The Grand runs not only through the Elora Gorge Park, with millions of trails, but into the old Elora Quarry, which is very deep, blue, clean and diveable from atop its 60-foot cliffs. Go watch the Elora kids do flips off the top — that is if you're too chicken to dive yourself! How to get to Elora? Take the 401 to Highway 6 north through Guelph, turn left on Wellington City Road 7 and follow the signs to Elora Gorge Conservation Area. Great hiking, hotels, B&Bs, restaurants and antique shops." — *HM*

Cheltenham Badlands • Up until this past weekend I'd never even heard of the Badlands, much less been cognizant of their location. Then, as Fortuna would have it, I spotted the great white blazes of the mighty Bruce Trail disappearing into the forest to the east, off the Creditview Road exactly 1K north of the Boston Mills Road, high up in the Caledon Hills. I get so excited when I spot a trail, my adrenaline hits the roof.

I found a parking spot up the way, pulled well off the road, backtracked to the trail and bounded headlong into the forest. No sooner was I firmly ensconced in bush than I came upon a blue sign describing the Russell Cooper Loop Trail, which took me up in those great humpy Caledon Hills and out onto a windy plateau of thorny trees and savannah scrub before descending onto the hard, red, terra-cotta clay of the Cheltenham Badlands — so hidden away, yet so easy to get to. An ocean of rounded, red, hard-clay prairie foothills, slashed and carved by water erosion into cowboy mesa-like ridges and deep box canyons. Olde Baseline Road runs along the north end of the badlands, and there's a parking lot to bring the older folks for a look. The windswept view gives you a 360-degree eyeful, with the Caledon Mountain and Devil's Pulpit on your north flank and the city of Mississauga far off in the southern sheen. The blue blazes of Bruce then took me over the Badland's rolling clay ocean, following the southwesterly ridge back to the mountain trail. I watched the angry wind whipping up the valley dust, roiling it like a corkscrew

Pen Pal: Slovenia Nadja

"I'm writing you from Slovenia. I sing in a choir and we are coming to Toronto in mid-October. We'll have some concerts on the weekends. We want to do some travelling during the weekdays. I was thinking about visiting a National Park or some special natural wonders of Canada and do some very easy hiking and have a picnic in nature. What could you suggest?" — *Nadja, Slovenia*

"Nadja, I would suggest a special trip for your choir to the Devil's Pulpit in Belfountain, which should be a healthy balance to all your church-going choir activities!" — *HM*

upwards through the cedars, and shooting the red powder back into the sky. The Cheltenham Badlands on the Russell Cooper Trail is a magnificent family hiking adventure. One hour tops. On my way back to the car I heard the trees moaning like a banshee, the howling wind moving them hither and yon. If you're looking for a longer boot, combine this one-hour hike with the Credit Stone loop continuing just to the west of Olde Baseline Road. The trail heads north into the Caledon Mountains and adds another hour of spice into the mix.

21 *The Double Bruce Mystery*

Fool me once — Shame on you.
Fool me twice — Shame on me.

I get all warm and fuzzy when I join up the dots and discover a new hiking trail. I finally pinned all four corners onto, without exaggeration, the finest, most arduous up-and-downhill hike this side of Vancouver's Grouse Grind.

I had been driven crazy for a decade each time I found myself in the Forks of the Credit Provincial Park, trying to follow the two main trails, both belonging to Bruce, both leading out of the park, heading south. One heads down MacLaren Road past the Forks Road, where the white blazes disappear up into the cedar and maple-sugar bush, while the other main trail leaves through the back door of the park, taking us down Dominion Street through the little town of Brimstone on the Credit River, and straight the hell up the Caledon Mountain to the top of the Devil's Pulpit. Both these white trails run parallel to each other 1K apart. Go figure!

I was stymied! And riding high on the turnip truck. That is, until November 8, 2000, when I belled the cat in Belfountain. What I didn't know was that MacLaren Road, which runs south from the Forks of the Credit Road, winds its languid way, switching back and forth, up the Caledon Mountain, where it eventually joins up with the other Bruce Trail at the Grange

Sideroad. Then both head west past the top of the Devil's Pulpit towards Mississauga Road, but not before cutting through the Cheltenham Badlands on the way to the Boston Mills Road. Eureka, Archimedes. I have found it!

This was our missing link, the key to the toughest, most visually delightful 90-minute hike around. The Big Square, starting at the corner of Creditview and Grange Sideroad, offers the hiker not one but two Bruce Trails. Park your car at the Grange Sideroad, head north up Creditview, and throw yourself over the 360-foot drop of the Devil's Pulpit, yet another suicide series of steps, ropes, rocks and handrails. If you actually make it to the bottom alive, walk out Chisolm Street to the river heading west, then north across the Forks humpy concrete bridge and up Dominion Street through the 200-year-old village of Brimstone to the provincial park gates and beyond. Once ensconced on the park trail, head up the big hill along the ridge, north to the ancient waterfall where 400-million years ago the Ordovician and Silurian land masses were married and mated. You may bear witness to their amorous couplings while reclining on rough-hewn wood benches, enjoying your apple and oysters and brie.

When you're ready to head back south, continue along the high ridge. But do not descend the big hill back down to the river from whence you came. Oh no! Soon you'll be following the white blazes of the second Bruce Trail, which will take you down a farmer's lane and then to MacLaren Street, south across the Forks Road to the little bridge. Just across the raging Credit, you'll see the Bruce disappearing up the 62 steps into the cedar ladies. The rest is easy. Jump off the Bruce onto the Grange Sideroad as it rises up to greet you again and follow it west to Creditview and back to your car. Take this book along with you and follow my directions assiduously, because it's all too much to remember.

This wonderful three-hour hike can be shortened by cutting across the Forks of the Credit Road from Chisolm to MacLaren, choosing not to go up Dominion Street into the park. Depending on your energy level on the day, you can either walk up the tortuous Pulpit or lazily meander down, all depending on which way you execute the square.

It's all here — a killer climb, a high-country sugar-bush trail, a Credit riverside pop through the cedar ladies, and a back-road country-concession stride. I've solved the Double Bruce Trail Mystery for all to enjoy.

So head up Mississauga Road to Grange Sideroad east to Creditview, and begin to solve the Double Bruce Trail Mystery for yourself. It may take you several tries, but who's in a hurry, eh?

22 *Mono Cliffs Provincial Park, Caledon Hills*

There's a magical little mountain village tucked away at the top of Airport Road. Mono Centre is not much bigger than a dozen old houses, restaurants, pub and bed and breakfast. But the centrepiece, the pot of gold, has to be Mono Cliffs Provincial Park, high up in the sky, where the Caledons and the Escarpment collide. You leave your car in town and start to hike north, when all of a sudden the path opens up into this giant sky valley surrounded by four mountains, with a jet stream kind of wind that screams and blusters over your head. Spectacular!

Then you climb the Escarpment and follow the cliff-edge trail. Staircases take you from the cliff top to escarpment face and glacial spillway through a gnarled and bent forest where the oldest trees in Ontario live — the 700-year-old eastern white pines.

Round trip, two hours, five stars. Take Airport Road north past Highway 9 for 40 miles, then go left on the 20th Sideroad, one block west to Mono Centre. Hiker Bob Lehman from Shelbourne recommended this trail. He insisted on it, and I'm glad he did. Better park up at the Mono Cliffs Outdoor Education Centre, much closer to the high cliffs, 1.5K north from the village centre on the 2nd Line. Go to Mono. You'll weep, it's so beautiful.

23 *The Caledon Quickie*

Remember the quickie? (Bet you haven't heard the word "quickie" in a year or two!) Can you recall those mid-day bouts of wild passion and physical abandonment, culminating in a blissful peace, tinged with light, sweet melancholy? The dangerous feeling usually comes upon you in the midst of a busy and constructive day, when it's almost impossible to find the time for dalliance of any kind. Most times, one dismisses the idea out of hand as inopportune. But every once in a while, the urge becomes so overwhelming that your mind races to find a way to work one in.

And so you clear the next two hours, as you and your special friend make a dash for your car, head out north of the airport on 427 to Highway 50 past Bolton, that almost perfectly sleepy Humber Valley town. You gun a left on Castlederg Road, and right onto Duffy's Lane, where you pull the car deeply into the vegetation, well off the shoulder of the northeast corner. Then, stripping off your work duds, you quickly slip into something a little more comfortable — your hiking clothes.

What lies ahead of you both over the next 60 minutes is pure physical pleasure. Fifteen minutes walking north on Duffy's hard-packed Caledon dirt road brings you to the welcoming wooden fence stile of the world-famous Humber Valley Heritage Trail, an early winner of the Golden Boot Award for Best

Damned Hiking Trail in the Megacity. This seldom-used grassy trail runs you south and east along the sparkly Humber riverside, through the languid, gossipy, cedar courtesans, and up into the thick, dark beech-tree forest, where the beaver family dines out nightly, then past the roiling limey soybean fields. And as if by magic, you find yourself thrust back onto Castlederg Road, and a short 10-minute jog east puts you back at your car in just under an hour, suitably sated and happily exhausted.

The Caledon Quickie is only two hours round trip from downtown Toronto. This back-road river-valley trail is both a great cardio workout and a never-ending series of visual orgasms. Quiet, pristine serenity in the middle of an otherwise hectic workday. Then you're back in the office before anyone knows you're gone. No one's the wiser, and nothing's changed, except for your fellow worker's comments on your pink, healthy afterglow and the crooked grin you just can't seem to wipe off your mug. Sounds pretty good, huh? Try a Caledon Quickie on for size. You'll find it a little tight for time at first, but since we only go 'round once, life is short, death is long — you know the rest. Party down, hikers. Try the quickie with your friend, but she's got to promise not to tell!

Pen Pal: Walking Charlotte

"Hi, Hiker Mike: I have friends from England who hope to come over next year. They belong to a walking group in England and were wondering if there is something similar here in Canada. Do you know of any organized group where they could go off for a few days in Ontario and walk? Yours very truly, Charlotte."

— *Oakville, Ontario*

"Dear Charlotte: There are myriad hiking clubs in the Megacity — Bruce Trail, Oak Ridges, Ganaraska — all of which lead hikes every day of the week. The Humber Valley Heritage Trail was built by a group of British volunteer engineer-hikers who came over and were billeted in Bolton homes while designing a heavenly trail along the Humber River. Your friends from 'jolly old England' will feel right at home."

— *HM*

24 *St. Patrick's Day Party Hike with Finnerty and Duffy*

There is an enchanting little village on the Humber River, just to the north of us, named Bolton, a place where Mother Nature lives in all her springtime glory. Bolton and her little sister village, Palgrave, home of the famous Palgrave Forest, are both rife with hiking trails for the outdoor enthusiast, from beginner to advanced. The Humber Valley Trail, winner of the 1998 Golden Boot Award, runs riverside north and connects with the mighty Bruce Trail in the Albion Hills Park, on its way to Palgrave, bisecting the Caledon Trailway, now a part of the 16,000K Trans Canada Trail. But it's to the deep-and-dark Palgrave Forest we've come to hike this morning, to the corner of Finnerty Sideroad and Duffy's Lane, in celebration of St. Patrick's Day. You can see the circumference trail running all the way 'round the forest, just through the fence at the crossroads. The path is soft and benign, and it will be an easy two hours back to your car.

Palgrave was re-forested with millions of pines back in the '30s and '40s to stem erosion of the Albion Hills, and it's just been recently that the Conservation Authority has started thinning out every other row, so the remaining pines can now breath a little easier and stretch out their branches to the sun. Palgrave trails are not maintained, so watch your step, or you'll be sorry!

What is it with animals, anyway? Why do they all like to poop smack dab in the middle of the trail? Dogs, deer, bear, raccoons and coyotes. They've got the whole forest to go in but "No," they must say to themselves, "let's go over to the path and show the humans what we've got." So tread lightly hikers. Another observation of note: I must have bumped into a dozen or so single males like myself out hiking with their dogs in this forest. We need more women hikers for balance in the Palgrave Forest.

Head up Highway 50 north from Highway 7 through Bolton

to Palgrave and Finnerty Sideroad. Turn left, or west, to Duffy's Lane and park. You'll see the Palgrave Trail on the left. Hike to your heart's content and say "God love ya" to Finnerty and Duff from Hiker Mike. And may the rest of you be in heaven half an hour before the Devil knows you're dead!

Pen Pal: Australian Danny

"How's it going, Hiker Mike? I recently arrived back home after spending a year in Australia. It was there that I discovered the wonderful world of bush walking. How would I go about getting trail maps? Thanks." — *Danny, West Rouge*

"Danny, Mountain Equipment Co-op has trail books and maps for the entire world. Topographicals from Energy, Mines and Resources are best for the Megacity — Brampton, Markham, Bolton and Toronto — at $9 each for the big picture. MEC costs $5 to join and also has the best deals in outdoor gear." — *HM*

25 *Primrose Julie*

Julie Underwood strikes again. That beautiful and mysterious eco-hiker from Andrews Scenic Acres out the Bruce Trail way has faxed me directions to what she considers to be one of the most beautiful hikes in Southern Ontario. It's called Primrose, in the Boyne River Valley.

Primrose is a pretty little village situated at the crossroads of Highway 10, north of Caledon, and Highway 89, east of Shelbourne. The length of the trek is 14K (five hours), and it's an easy-to-moderate loop that passes through Boyne Valley Provincial Park. I'm going out early tomorrow morning with a bunch of the Urban Sherpas and will report back to you next week on what we find.

Thank you Julie, who also told us about the Mansfield-Dufferin Forest hike, which appears in the *Best Hikes* book.

26 *The Primrose Trail*

Very recently, I had the distinct pleasure of visiting Mother Nature's strip joint, called Weather in the Raw. The Primrose Section of the Bruce Trail dirtily dances her way up to the top of Murphy's Pinnacle, the great, double camel-back bosoms of sand and gravel some 200 feet in the sky. Then she dashes you down into Dante's Seventh Circle of Cedar Marsh Hell along the spectacular Boyne River. All in the hiking space of two hours time.

The blue blazes of the Primrose Section start just a mile north of Highway 89 on Dufferin 19 Road, which is simply the Mulmur Township name for our own Highway 10, about an hour north of Brampton and the 401. Access the Primrose to the east where the sign says "To Murphy's Pinnacle," and 20 minutes of vertical maple-bush trail later you're standing on the top of Ontario. When I was there, the wind was so

Pen Pal: Smitten Nancy Ball

"Dear Hiker Mike: I would like to take up hiking. My husband has taken up mountain biking. Although I've tried it, I seem to be pushing my bike up a lot of hills instead of riding, so I thought hiking would really be of great interest to me. I walk approximately 30 to 35K a week, and quite frankly I'm tired of walking around the community I live in. I really enjoy being in the forested areas, hills, etc.... What would you suggest regarding a hiking club. I live in Richmond Hill and would be going on my own as none of my friends want to 'walk that far.' Thanks."

— *Nancy Ball, Richmond Hill, Ontario*

"Your e-mail was featured last Saturday morning on the show, when I told you to call Harold Sellers at Hike Ontario at 416-426-7391 and ask him if you can join the Oak Ridges Trail Club, running east-west directly south of Richmond Hill. Hikes go out four times a week and the hike leaders are great people. Report back on your adventure." — *HM*

strong that I had to crouch down in the lee to write this part of the report, but boy was it worth the hike to the top! Total 360-degree view. Mulmur and Dufferin Townships — a veritable checkerboard of working farms and hundreds of conifer forests patchworking their way towards the horizon's big curve. Magnifico!

Descending the Pinnacle, you'll find that the trail heads parallel to the Boyne River Valley just above, staying to the high pasture ground, heading east, smack through an old apple orchard. Here it was almost December, but the apples I picked from the trees were crunchy, sharp, and sweet to the taste.

Use the stiles over the field fences as you pass through the working farms. Look for the doggy hole next to the stile or lift the fence up gently so Bowser can slip under, then replace the fence carefully.

The eastern trail soon T-bones with the north-south white blazes of the main trail of the Bruce, which means it's time to head south — I mean way south — into the Valley of the Boyne. You'll follow the farmer's two-rut tractor trail. The contrast to the howling of the Aeolian wind, kindred spirit to the Caledon's craggy peaks, is the stunningly quiet and peaceful serenity of the Boyne River Valley — all dark green, lushy mushy, and rife with spongy old-growth forest moss, which takes over 100 years to grow properly, and the darkly clear, fast-flowing Boyne River, over which passes a 40-foot, well-crafted wooden bridge built by trail volunteers.

There must have been a terrible storm through this area recently, because there are hundreds of cedars ripped right out of the ground and lying across the trail. So you'll have to pay close attention to the white blazes ahead of you, because the trail really wants to play hide and seek down by the river.

The Boyne River–Primrose Trail spills out onto Highway 89 and Hurontario at the southeast point of the loop. But you don't have to take 89 back to your car. Just behind you in the bush 100 yards or so is a farmer's snowmobile trail running west through fields all the way back to Highway 10 and Prince of Wales, making for the perfect two-hour loop through beautiful

country. But it's arduous, hikers, all that vertical work with the Pinnacle way up high and the Boyne way down low. Take plenty of water, your heavy boots and your cell phone. Give yourself plenty of time to complete the Primrose loop, which in its entirety is 14K and will take you a good five hours. But who's counting!

Thank you once again, Julie Underwood, for showing me another stunning Dufferin Townships hike.

Pen Pal: Nancy Ball, Totally, Awesomely Smitten

"Dear Hiker Mike: I just got back from a five-day trip to Mount Tremblant. I biked about 30 to 40K a day, but on the last day, I told my husband I was going to hike up Mount Tremblant. Everyone said I should do the green, easy way up trail, but I wanted a real hike . . . so I'm happy to report to you that I hiked up the Black Diamond Trail to the top of Mount Tremblant, and did it in two hours. I am truly thrilled, and now for sure I know hiking is for me. It was rated a 'strenuous' hike, and there was a lot of climbing, however being in the forest and observing the nature was so calming and peaceful that every time we would take a water break or a quick snack I was just overwhelmed at how beautiful the scenery was. We observed two very large deer on the path just in front of us and fortunately, no bears. . . . I've just never been so proud of myself. Thanks Hiker Mike, all I kept saying to my husband was 'I can hardly wait to tell Hiker Mike that I did it!' Today Mount Tremblant, tomorrow. . . ? Who knows! Sincerely," — *Nancy Ball, Richmond Hill, Ontario*

"Don't look now, Nancy, but I think you just fell in love — with hiking."

— *HM*

27 *The Oak Ridges Moraine*

The Oak Ridges Moraine has been in the news quite a bit lately. Recent attempts to develop those great huge humps and bumps of sand and gravel spanning the top of Toronto have been met with furious opposition, thanks to the hikers and environmentalists who want to maintain the Moraine's ecology and scenic integrity.

When the Wisconsin Glacier melted some 10,000 years ago, it left behind a massive ridge of hummocky mini mountains, interspersed with kettle lakes, extending 160K from the Niagara Escarpment in the west to the Trent River watershed in the east. Apart from farmland, the area is covered with thick deciduous bush of maple and oak and conifers, spruce and cedar. Next time you drive north out of Toronto notice that you're going forever uphill to Major MacKenzie, Stouffville, Aurora and Newmarket. This is our very own Oak Ridges Moraine, on top of which, running east to west, is the stunningly beautiful Oak Ridges Trail. The trail is marked with white blazes painted on trees, rocks, fences and stiles, and runs through local conservation areas such as the Goodwood, Claremont and Glen Major, all of which offer treetop views of the Toronto skyline and Lake Ontario.

The Oak Ridges Trail Association is headed up by Hike Ontario executive members Fiona Cowles, Bob Ellison and my old pal, happy Harold Sellers, the friendliest guy on the Oak Ridges Trail. This gang has just published an amazing *Oak Ridges Trail Guidebook*, complete with a living history of the trail and all the trail information you'll need, including a series of seven

Pen Pal: Steve, and the Langstaff Eco Hike

"Dear Hiker Mike: My wife and I discovered a wonderful little hiking trail today. It's called the 'Langstaff Eco-Park' and its trailhead is situated at the southwest corner of Highway 7 and North Rivermede Road, located across the road from a McDonald's. I think it is an underused little gem, which goes about 2K north from its start and has a wide gravel path almost its entire length, so it's good for grannies. The pretty path does wind through some woods, but mostly meadow and marshland. There's a wonderful little pond with an overlook and plaques that describe the genesis of the trail. It's certainly not a wilderness experience, lots of factories not too far away, but very peaceful anyway. Some interesting sights too; look for the old windmill. The trail ends at Langstaff Road. On the way back we came upon a big old painted turtle ambling along the path, and to our surprise a beautiful deer leapt across the path not more than 10 feet in front of us. Took us about an hour to do the hike at a leisurely pace and we didn't come across another soul. Let me know if you try out this little trail. — Cheers." — *Steve Salkovitch, Thornhill, Ontario*

"Thanks for the new trail, Steve. Consider yourself an honourary Urban Sherpa." — *HM*

removable waterproof maps to take with you on your hike, all for $20. The *Trail Guide* can be purchased at Mountain Equipment Co-op, or you can call Harold Sellers at 905-853-3518, and while you're at it, why not pick up a family membership?

The Wisconsin Glacier's recession left in its wake tremendous biodiversity for us to enjoy while we hike the Comeback Trail to Fitness. But we must preserve the ecosystem for future generations. We can all do our part to protect the Moraine by becoming a member of the trail club and by pledging $10 each to the Oak Ridges Moraine Land Trust, Box 577, Aurora, Ontario L4G 3L6. If everyone who lives on or near the Moraine, and hikers who use the trail, gave ten bucks each, we would have enough money to buy the land, thus making sure that the uninterrupted green corridor running across the top of Toronto would be there for our kids and grandkids.

28 *North Road Allowance: The Garbage Hike*

Hiker Mike's on a Sunday morning cast-about — looking for hiking trouble. The Big Snoop! Cruising out the 401 east, I see a sign for Brock Road, named after that English renegade warrior and explorer. Sounds perfect! So I head north into the Oak Ridges Moraine with the Seaton Trail and the Duffins Creek on my left until I reach Concession 7, and turning west, I spot North Road heading, you guessed it, north into the bush with a "No Exit" sign beckoning to me.

North Road isn't a road as such, more a farmer's lane heading up between the fields — two tractor ruts surrounded by a healthy cacophony of crows and small airplane engines. I park the car at the concrete abutment and follow the fresh ATV tracks in the light dust of snow up a lane of gnarled old fruit trees and an old pine agreement forest, and just as I'm getting into the nature serenity groove, I trip over a load of garbage that some lazy moron found was easier to dump in the bush than having to pay the two bucks at the township. I feel sorry for the poor farmer as he tries to manoeuvre his tractor around the mountains of shingles, old furniture and kitchen appliances on his way to spring planting. No wonder landowners don't want to give permission for hiking trails through their property. So hikers, when possible, pick up what litter you can to make the earth a little better for your having been there.

Continuing north the trail gets rougher, with branches down across the way. You'll cross the tracks and follow the contour and hump of the old road through a beautiful pasture of cedar and maple, freshly adorned with lovely old living room furniture grouped around a campfire, loose tires for coffee tables and lots of beer bottles. But just past the party pasture, the pathway widens into a hard-packed, well-used road heading north with a great vista of the Oak Ridges. We turn right onto Concession Road 2 past Little Red Brick Schoolhouse No.16, built in 1864, on the banks of the Duffins Creek.

I did try to find the Seaton Trail, but it looks as if it doesn't

come this far north, so I crossed the Duffins bridge and headed east to Sideroad 29. With a warm southerly breeze kissing my face, I headed back down into the morning sun, Concession 7, and my car.

The North Road Allowance, north off Concession 7, is a pretty rough go, with some bushwhacking required. But as more and more of us use it, the trail will gentle up. Just be quiet and polite passing private property. Always wave and say "Hi" to the landowners as you pass. You are Toronto's hike ambassadors to the world.

29 *Stouffville–Uxbridge Hiking*

Here's another great Oak Ridges hike out between Stouffville and Uxbridge. It's a little complicated to get to, so read carefully.

Find yourself on the Bloomington Sideroad and the 10th Line, which both meet with the York-Durham Line. Follow the York-Durham Road south exactly 8K, and the trail is on your left. The world-famous Oak Ridges Trail heads east into the cedar bush just to the north of a pretty lake with an A-frame cottage on an island. Be prepared for a low-down wetland bog crossing. Wear your waterproof high tops because it's a good 100 metres across the bog to achieve the high ground on the other side.

Early spring is really no time to be in the bush, what with the muck and ice and dead leaves underfoot. But what else are you going to do with all that springtime testosterone sap running through your veins? Don't get me started!

A good way to blow off all the energy is by hitting the bush. Because the springtime trails are wet and splooshy, the tendency is to move way off the centre of the pathway up to drier ground. But by doing this you end up destroying the poor vulnerable little plants and flowers who were living happily on the side of the path until you came along and trampled them to death underfoot. So please be aware as you're moving through them.

The trail finally evened out just as I leapt the CNR tracks crossing the trail. It was then that I was smacked in the eyeballs by Mother Nature's movie — a magnificent triple-trunk willow tree reaching out across the trail to greet me in a most accommodating manner. And under it flowed a busy little springtime brook, chatting merrily to anyone who'd stop to listen. The Oak Ridges Trail is exceedingly well marked; large white blazes on trees make sure you never get that queasy where-the-hell-am-I feeling, when the trail markings dry up and disappear.

I finally reached a 50-foot-wide mud bath of a road that some insensitive Oak Ridges developer had bulldozed through the bush, impeding my progress. I was forced to turn around and head back. Now that really burns me! No consideration for your fellows. I guess you can tell on which side of the fence I stand in this Oak Ridges overdevelopment debacle.

The Oak Ridges Moraine is the source of all of the river valleys running down into Lake Ontario. Let's try and hold onto her beauty for as long as we can so our kids and grandkids can play in the bush just like us.

30 *Bruce King Eulogy: An Oak Ridges Tragedy*

Hiking is a wonderful sport: not only do we satisfy the urge to explore the forests and river valleys, we also get the chance to make our bodies better and our minds sharper, and to fill our spirits to the brim with the joy of life. But sometimes the trails are fraught with danger, so we must prepare for the unexpected.

On Wednesday, September 13, 2000, you'll all remember, we were visited by violent weather. Horizontal lightning flashed across the top of Toronto, turning the skies black and the trails into mud slides. Veteran trekkers Harold Sellers and Robert Ellison took 14 hikers out along the King Section of the Oak Ridges Trail, south of Pottageville, and soon found themselves bombarded by the monsoon rainstorm. Somewhere deep in the forest, away from civilization, one of the Wednesday regulars, Hiker Bruce King from Markham, stepped off the trail on a switchback to catch his breath and suddenly collapsed. CPR was applied immediately, as Harold tried to phone for help, but the cell phones didn't work in the forest. Although Robert ran out to the road in the driving rain, flagging down a truck to take him to a house to call an ambulance, it was too late by the time the medics got back to Bruce. The whole event was very traumatic for all concerned.

Thank goodness there were hikers present who were able to administer CPR to the fallen hiker — men and women who were trained to help on the trail. And it's just this kind of training that Hike Ontario offers in their leadership training course. We've got to be prepared for unfortunate and tragic events on the trail.

Bruce King died that Wednesday, deep in the forest, high up in the Oak Ridges Moraine. Don't you find it ironic, but altogether appropriate, that Bruce King's final living hours should be spent on the King Section of the Oak Ridges Trail? Hike on, Bruce King, wherever you may be. We'll all miss you.

If you'd like to enroll in Hike Ontario's Hike Leadership Training Program, call 416-426-7362, and be prepared the next time misfortune finds you on the trail of life.

31 *West Rouge Jr. Public School*

A couple of weeks ago, my teacher friend Dorie Preston and her Grade 5 class invited me out to their West Rouge Jr. Public School to talk about hiking, both here in Toronto and around the world. Places exotic, like Nepal, the Annapurna Sanctuary, the Everest Base Camp Trek, and closer to home, the Mayan Pathways along the Yucatan Jungle Peninsula of southern Mexico. I spent an wonderful hour with these bright, energetic kids, whose questions were candid, frank and very succinct. "How sick did you really get climbing up to Base Camp?"

These Grade 5ers had inquiring minds and really wanted to know. Just like every final exam I've ever had — Hikes Around the World, compare and contrast. Didn't you just hate that? When the only question on the page was "The Renaissance in Italy and the Reformation in Europe; compare and contrast." Where, in heaven's name, does one begin?

And so, compare and contrast we did. Now most of these kids haven't yet hiked the far-flung trails around the globe, but don't forget, these Grade 5ers live in the Rouge River Valley, and take it from Hiker Mike, there is no place more beautiful than our very own Carolinian Sun Pocket — the Rouge — stretching from Reesor Road and Steeles in the north, down past the Zoo and Pearce House on the Vista Ridge and Orchard Trails, past Sheppard Avenue and Twin Rivers Drive along the riverside trail, past the campgrounds on Kingston Road, all the way along the marshes to Lake Ontario.

Imagine growing up in such a wilderness. Needless to say, the kids of the West Rouge Jr. Public School and I had much to discuss. As a follow-up activity, the kids produced their own "Best Hikes Book," a bound collection of postcard-sized sketches of the nature trails of all their favourite hiking destinations, with not only the Rouge but also the Blue Mountain trails in Collingwood, the forest and pathways out Peterborough and Lindsay way, and waterfront trails around Pigeon Lake.

So thank you Tori, Julia, Vini, Kaitlin, Samantha, Meghan, Jason, Matthew, Scott, Katie, Leanne, Travis, Jay, Elyse, Jordan, Phil, Kevin and anyone else I missed. And carry your love of hiking and the outdoors with you forever. Then pass it on to your kids.

After spending that hour comparing and contrasting all the different hikes around the world, those Rouge Valley kids and I came to the same conclusion: "There's no place like home, Dorie. There's no place like home."

32 *Rouge Valley: Bear Mountain*

Yesterday morning Captain Karl and I went in search of Canada's largest wind turbine out in Pickering. We wanted a view of the big windmill that would put it into perspective — all 117 metres of her. So we drove out the 401 east to Meadowvale and headed north to the Zoo entrance, but instead of going west into the animals, we turned east into Rouge Park at Pearce House.

We parked our car and hiked due east along the asphalt to the top of the Bear Mountain landfill site, which took about a half hour, and when we got to the top of the winding road we could see the entire 11,500 acres of Rouge Park, the largest inner-city park in North America. And right down along the shore of Lake Ontario stood the biggest, whitest bird I've ever seen — the Wind Turbine — shimmering white-gold in the sun and ready to fly.

Take the whole family for a hike up Bear Mountain, the view is magical, or drive to the bottom of Brock Road to see it up close.

ASSAULT ON ALGONQUIN

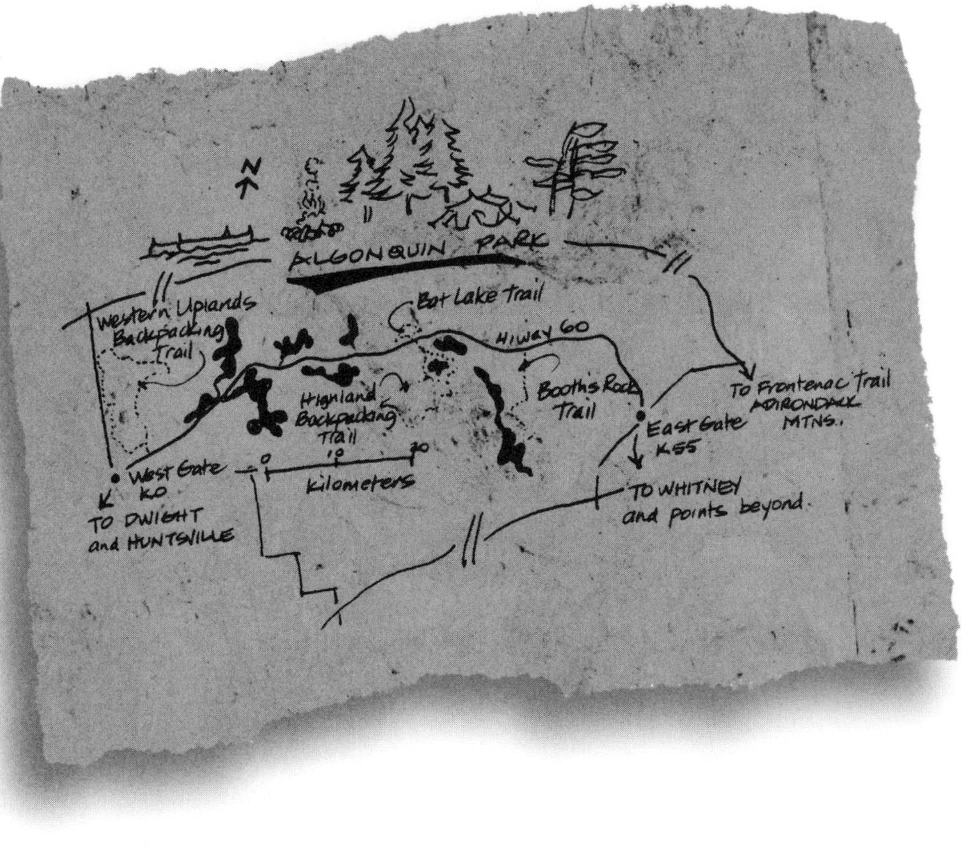

Pen Pal: Canada Backpacking

"A friend and I are looking to plan a backpacking trip in Canada. We wish to have no contact with the outside world, to marvel at the wonders of nature for a week or so. Do you have any ideas for us? We live in Massachusetts. Thanks." —*Joe, Massachusetts, USA*

"For summer adventures with a backpack, call Killarney Provincial Park at 705-287-2900, Temagami at 705-569-3791 or Algonquin Park and Lake Superior Provincial Park at 1-888-668-7275. Also, Bushwacker Boris has winter adventures for the stout-at-heart voyageur. Journey on snowshoes through the land of Grey Owl, hauling your gear on sleds and toboggans. Sleep in canvas tents heated by sheet-metal stoves. Call Boris at *Bushwacker*, at 705-435-1211. He'll either kill you, or show you a grand time in the wilderness!" —*HM*

33 *The Day Hiker's Guide to the Bush Trails of Algonquin Park*

A nasty wind slapped the driving rain into my windshield as I drove up the side of the Don Valley on Pottery Road, barely able to see the centre line. The inclemency of the late fall weather did not bode well for the upcoming weekend assault on Algonquin Park, some three hours north of Big Smoke. I was on my way to pick up old pal and Urban Sherpa Hiking Club captain Karl Pruner, who had agreed to help me notch up the last two-day hikes needed for the book.

There's nothing like starting a day without sunlight. I find the time before dawn to be most depressing, especially in bad weather, but the entire ugly scenario changed on a dime when the good Captain barged down his front walkway, hefted his two large backpacks and hiking stick into the back seat and slid into shotgun position while wishing me a great and glorious "Good morning!" It was as if the sun had just come out.

After stopping for large lattes at Timothy's, we set a new land-speed record on the 400 Highway between Toronto and the

Huntsville cut-off to Highway 60. Two hours flat. And 30 minutes later, we stepped into the Algonquin Park headquarters for our $10 parking permits and brochures and directions to the trailheads that we had planned to hike.

Algonquin Park is the ultimate in planning and execution. Not only are the trails divided into backpacking and camping trails, the Park also features fourteen day hikes as well, for outdoor people not planning on staying overnight. Three kinds of day hikes are featured and spelled out in the brochures conveniently displayed under the big map at each trailhead. Most hikes deliver you to fantastic high-in-the-sky lookouts with an area to rest and picnic while surveying the patchwork of forest and lakes far below. Some hikes will take you through history by way of ruins, estates, mills and camps. Ecologically sensitive areas are featured, along with places guaranteed to give you wildlife encounters. The day-hiking terrain can be straight up or gradual to the mountain tops, or flat as a pancake through the lakes and portages, with long, wooden walkways over the bogs. Hiking times range from two to six hours.

You can hardly get lost in Algonquin Park, as the day-hiking trails are clearly marked with large blue plastic circles nailed nicely to the trees at eye level. The great bonus is the brochure you pick up at the trailhead. It's a play-by-play of the hike and is meant to be read while taking the hike, much like the audio

narration you receive while walking through the Sistine Chapel in the Vatican. The whole hike is spelled out for you, bunky, blow by blow.

Over the past two years, we've hiked both the Western Uplands and the Highlands backpacking trails, which we found long and arduous. This is because one is meant to stop and camp every few Ks, not run the length in seven hours. And that's what makes these day hikes so attractive. You can take your time, knowing full well that completion must come before sunset, so there is no danger of ending up lost and alone with night falling. Or you can literally run the route in record time for the ultimate cardiovascular workout. As you will discover, there is an Algonquin day hike for every energy level, and the brochure will make it very clear to you exactly what you're getting into. So very sophisto!

Take the Algonquin Park experience a few rungs up the ladder. Do a little research by purchasing the bible: *The Algonquin Park Visitor's Guide*, by the park ranger himself, Wayne Van Sickle. The history, the wildlife, the canoeing, backpacking and day hiking are all there, and it's published not only in our mother tongue but in German as well. The guide is under $20 and is published by Stone Cutter Press.

I met Wayne at a book signing in Norval on the Credit River during the Springtime Riverfest Festival some years back. We had a ball talking each other's book up to potential buyers. Wayne and I exchanged books at the end of the day, and Wayne's inscription to me was, "Come hiking with me and the black flies in Algonquin any time." I did the next best thing! I'm using his wonderful book and self-educating at my own pace.

34 *Booth's Rock: The Sprint*

Inside the Algonquin Park Visitor's Guide are fourteen day hikes, two of which the Captain and I enjoyed this past weekend.

The Booth's Rock Trail, at three hours and 5K, was the first. We arrived at the trailhead along with a busload of hikers from Toronto's Stroll in the Park Hiking Club. Although we greeted all 50 of the hikers with a pleasant word as we were passing them, we succeeded in leaving them well behind as we sprinted up the side of the mountain and into the thick, dark, quiet forest. This initial adrenaline rush of getting away from the horde stayed with us for the entire hike. Even as we stood on the high ridge of Booth's Rock looking out over the lake-forest panorama, we were itching to keep moving. The trail is a large, banana-shaped loop to the top of the rock, then a big dive down the other side by way of a thousand-stepped staircase. After checking out the remains of an estate once occupied by a powerful judge, an old, flat railway line sprints you back along the lake under the brow of Booth's Rock high up on your right flank. Wayne's time is three hours in the book and he rates the hike as strenuous. Because of our energy on the day, we halved the time and found the trail to be a walk in the park. So you will probably fall somewhere in the middle when you ascend Booth's Rock, one of the finest lookouts in Algonquin Park.

How to get there? Once inside the Park, go to kilometre 40 on Highway 60 and head south exactly 8K.

35 *Bat Lake: Walking on Water*

After nailing Booth's Rock Hike to the wall in an hour and a half, we changed out of our sweaty clothes back at the car, made a quick lunch of mackerel fillets, apples and iceberg water, then drove over to kilometre 30 and our afternoon hike along Bat Lake Trail. Wayne has it rated easy, flat and just under 6K — the kind of hike we were looking for in order to wind down from the morning sprint up Booth's Rock, and to stretch out our leg muscles and joints on level ground, while not having to pay as much attention to every footfall.

Bat Lake Trail nudges you into a filmy pine and mossy forest chock full of quiet, with a soft and spongy pathway perfect for a coureurs de bois's moccasins. There are some hills through the upland sugar-maple forest, but by and large the hike is a sturdy beginner's trek, and an easy leg for the experienced trekker.

If you are just becoming a hiker, set your own pace. Most important, make the hike a pleasure, not a chore. When you find yourself breathing a little too hard going uphill, stop and take a big break! God, hikers, if it ain't fun, why do it?

When we hit the boardwalk heading out across the acid lake, created not by man but by the black spruce, the rain made the waves wash across the wooden walkway as we went. There was just enough bounce in the boardwalk out in the middle to cause the water to sploosh up between the wood slats, giving us pause. From a distance, we must have looked like we were striding out across the top of Bat Lake, walking on top of the water.

After completing the Bat Lake loop in an hour or so, we jumped in the car and three hours later were back in Big Smoke in time for dinner and dancing around the living room with Libby and the Three Babes. The whole assault on the day hiking trails of Algonquin Park took exactly twelve hours. What do you think of that?

The following hikes are on backpackers' trails, much different in time and terrain. Plan for the whole day on some of these giant loops — three or four hours of morning hiking, stop for lunch and a swim, then the afternoon trek back out of the woods. The campsites on the backpacker's trails are magnificent: large, leafy clearings for your tent; giant fire pit; an actual outhouse toilet; and the finest sandy beach for swimming you'll find anywhere in North America. You might even consider strapping on your backpack, tent, food and pots and pans and trying that crazy backpacking sport for yourself. Stranger things have happened in the magical forests, lakes and mountains of Algonquin.

36 *The Highland Backpacking Trail*

Dropped into the Lake of Herbs and Spices for some healthy Haliburton hiking, we headed deep into the bush to strike a trail into Algonquin Park. Let me tell you what took place on a high, bright, sunny day in blue September. But before I do, I have to confide in you that this was only my second visit to the great provincial park just to the east of Huntsville on Highway 60, the technicolor trail that takes you clear through. The first time, we hiked the Western Uplands Backpackers Trail — 3½ hours into Maggie Lake, for lunch, a swim and a snooze, then 3½ hours back out to our car and home in time for *Monday Night Football.*

This time we chose the Highlands Backpackers Trail, some 31K east of the ticket cabin on Highway 60 — oh yeah, that's right, it'll cost you $10 to hike in Algonquin Park, and make sure you display the damnable ticket on your car windshield or they'll whack you upside the head with a $25 fine. Hey, small price to pay for one amazing vertical hike.

The Highlands Trail started climbing at the parking lot and didn't level off for about an hour, but once on top we rode astride a series of pink granite whale backs — huge, honking smooth stones outcropping the top of the mountains like breaching humpbacks. If you stay on the Highlands for two hours, you'll end up at a bunch of beachside campsites stretching around the very beautiful, still and serene Provoking Lake, a perfect four-hour backpacking destination. You see, hikers, we were booting it in light running shoes — *coureurs de bois* style — moving through the forest at 5K an hour, twice the speed of backpackers, carrying nothing but water and chocolate. We can do between three and four hours without a serious break and cover a greater distance with ease and alacrity.

This kind of hiking came out of years of running the 10K which, I'm convinced, is the best distance for physical fitness that lends itself to today's "hurry up and go" society. And Algonquin trails are the best trails for this kind of booting — wide and secure, well-marked and maintained, covered with a hard dirt-and-pine-needle mix, fully anchored by tree roots that form step-like ladder footings up and down the sides of the mountains. We took 20 minutes at Lake Provoking for a swim, then booted it out to Highway 60 in two more exciting hours, retracing our steps on the Highlands Trail, and were back in the car heading for New York sirloin steak and baked potatoes back at Beechman Gary's Hideout on Big Herb. Hikers, get up off your butts and go hike Algonquin, you've got a national treasure two hours north of Toronto and it's shouting for you to put your boots to it.

Directions are as follows. Take Highway 400 to Highway 11 north to Huntsville. Head east on Highway 60 to Algonquin Park

and call me in the morning. This is serious 180-beat-per-minute up-down booting that will keep the cardiovascular factory open for four hours. The toxins will run screaming from every pore of your body and you'll once again be as pure as the driven snow on your first Holy Communion Day. Algonquin Park rocks and rules. Attack it with all your energy, enthusiasm and gusto because hiking, my friends, is your ticket to a happy and healthy old age.

37 *Maggie Lake for Lunch*

reprinted from Hiker Mike's Best Hikes

Got a call from my old Urban Sherpa pal Beechman Gary. He missed his week on the Athabaska River because of the Air Canada strike and decided instead to treat us both to the Western Uplands Trail hike in Algonquin Park. So no sooner did we finish our hosting duties at the United Way Walk-a-Thon than up the big highway we go to Huntsville — turn right and head east on Highway 60. And just before the Algonquin gates we stopped at the Timber Trail cottages for a trout dinner, hiking preparations and a good night's sleep. They must have seen us coming because they charged us $150 for a dumpy little cabin with a black-and-white TV in the off-season. Shame on you, Timber Trail. We'll not be by again.

Woke up at 6 AM to the smell of Beachman's toast and coffee and the miserable sounds of rain, which turned to a cold drizzle, then stopped altogether by the time we got to the Western Uplands trailhead just inside Algonquin Park. We knew we were about to spend 8 to 10 rigorous hours in the bush. Western Uplands Trail is rugged mountain terrain designed for backpackers in extremely good condition, used to hiking 15 to 25K per day.

The trail was wide and gracious, well marked with blue and white backpacker's signs every 50 feet or so. Then we hit the first hill (mountain, more like it), straight up into the forest. I was thankful to be carrying a 15-pound daypack instead of 45 pounds of backpack. The work of the trail maintenance crew was the best I've seen. All brush and fallen trees chain-sawed away from the trail, no overhang, bridges cut from pine and cedar logs in 4-foot lengths. Atop the mountains are rest stops, large smooth rocks where you can sit and rest without taking off the backpack, and the cleared trail was a foot-happy mix of loamy humus and pine needle.

About 90 minutes into the hike, the Western Uplands Trail turns off into a side trail of beautifully designed campsites surrounding crystal-clear, sandy-bottomed Maple Leaf Lake. That's the destination for most day-hikers. But keep to the main trail, towards Maggie Lake, unless you want a swim, because you give up a lot of hard-earned high ground by heading down to the lake.

The section from Maple Leaf to Maggie Lake — two hours — is beyond the average hiker. Forget the Fitness Institute. Your pulse will be hitting 180 beats per minute trekking up these hills. You'll be energized if you're in top shape and you'll hit the golden groove. No mountain too high. The Body Factory open for business. Once past Maple Leaf, the trail roughens up and tapers off. It's rocky, less sure-footed, and dangerous. This is big-league hiking. Total silence. Only the birds, the breathing, the boots and the bears.

We eventually did climb up into and around the other side of stunningly pristine Maggie Lake, found a waterfront campsite, light an fire to make some soup, hit the water for a cool-down, enjoyed a lunch of oysters smoked with chocolate and oranges, located a comfy sunspot on pine needles, and snoozed for an hour. On our way back, we recognized landmarks we'd missed on the way up. One to look for is the world's most perfect Tom Thomson island, sitting pretty in the middle of Steep Rise Lake. Hikers, you'll want to move there. It's heaven smiling on a little piece of earth. You're looking at eight solid hours in the bush. This ain't no waltz in the Black Forest.

It was mid-September when we hiked the Western Uplands Trail, and we passed loads of backpackers. Fall's the best time to go. Winter is impossible, spring too muddy, and the bugs make you a banquet in summer. And a tip of the hiker fedora to Gary Beechey for showing us the magic of Algonquin.

38 *Bushwacker*

Bushwacker magazine is Ontario's authoritative outdoor hiking and canoeing voice, and the voice belongs to my old pal Bushwacker himself, Boris Swidersky. Boris has hiked, snowshoed, skied and canoed most everywhere in Canada, and now he's going to take us with him on his wilderness adventure trips, and not only in summer. The exploration trips involve backpacking, winter camping, bushwhacking and canoeing, and the cost to go is $50 a day (either bring your own food, or pay your share of the food costs). The groups will be kept small — no more than six people — and the first Bushwacker winter adventure begins in February, heading to Killarney Provincial Park, one of Ontario's most beautiful.

Then in March, journey to the Land of Grey Owl. In the northern town of Sudbury, we board the train that takes us into the back-country wilderness of Spanish Forest. You'll travel on snowshoes, hauling your gear on toboggans and sleds and sleeping in canvas tents heated by sheet-metal stoves. These adventures are not for sissies. Oh no! This is the genuine article, hikers. The Real Magilla. Contact Boris at 705-435-1566, or via bushwacker@sympatico.ca.

39 *Share the Trail*

There has been a great deal of talk lately about the Trans Canada Trail — a coast-to-coast hiking right-of-way linking thousands of communities across Canada. When completed, the Trans Canada Trail will lay claim to being the longest trail in the world, accommodating not only walkers, hikers, backpackers, cross-country skiers, dog sleds and horseback riders, but all-terrain vehicles and snowmobiles as well.

It's the collective work of all these sports clubs that will go into the successful completion of the trail. But already we're starting to hear from certain purist segments in Southern Ontario, objecting to the shared use of the trail with the noisy and intrusive engine-driven machinery that can be heard coming up behind the silent and serene hiker for miles (or kilometres). We've heard hikers complain bitterly about the noise and the supposed danger of speed and roll-over of the machines, and how snowmobiles are purported to chase down deer and moose and other game in the Far North. What we fail to see here in Southern Ontario is that ATVs and snowmobiles are an established way of life in the North.

Folks use ATVs to get to work, to go see their neighbours and friends, and to travel from town to town through the backwoods. Most of the northern trails were created, not by hikers and backpackers, but by snowmobile clubs, which charge their members substantial fees for trail use and maintenance. That's why there's a "user pay for hiking trails" movement afoot right now across the province. Most hikers get their backs up at the idea of user pay. They swear they will never pay for the privilege of walking through the woods, but like everything else in life, you gotta pay if you want to play.

Not long ago, I found myself on a wonderful trail running south from Dorset, in Haliburton, through the forest to the little town of Minden, some 20 to 30K to the south. The trail was

hard-packed, blazes and signs leading the way — even picnic tables, fire pits and outhouses every few kilometres. And the reason the trail was so good underfoot was because I was walking on a snowmobile trail.

The Trans Canada Trail will use existing pathways, old railway lines, logging roads and four-wheel-drive forest roads to link up the 16,000K trail from St. John's, Newfoundland, to Victoria, B.C., to Tuktoyaktuk in the Arctic, and if we want to make it work, we're all going to have to be most tolerant in sharing the trail with everyone. Although I have never been on a snowmobile, and never intend to use one myself, most every snowmobiler I have met on the trail has greeted me with a wave and a smile. That's enough for me. And it's also reassuring to know that when hiking in the middle of nowhere, there might be someone to come along who could help in case of an accident. Remember the Bruce King incident along the Oak Ridges Trail?

Not long ago, a rookie dog-sled racer lost his way for six days in Alaska's Caribou Hills. He survived by burying himself under his dogs for warmth and sharing their food until he was found by a group of local snowmobilers who just happened to be passing by. Thank goodness for ATVs on the Trans Canada Trail. Musher Rod Boyce owes his life to snowmobilers. Which goes to show, like Burton Cummings sings, "Baby, I'll be there to share the land." Let's all share the trails together.

TEMAGAMI

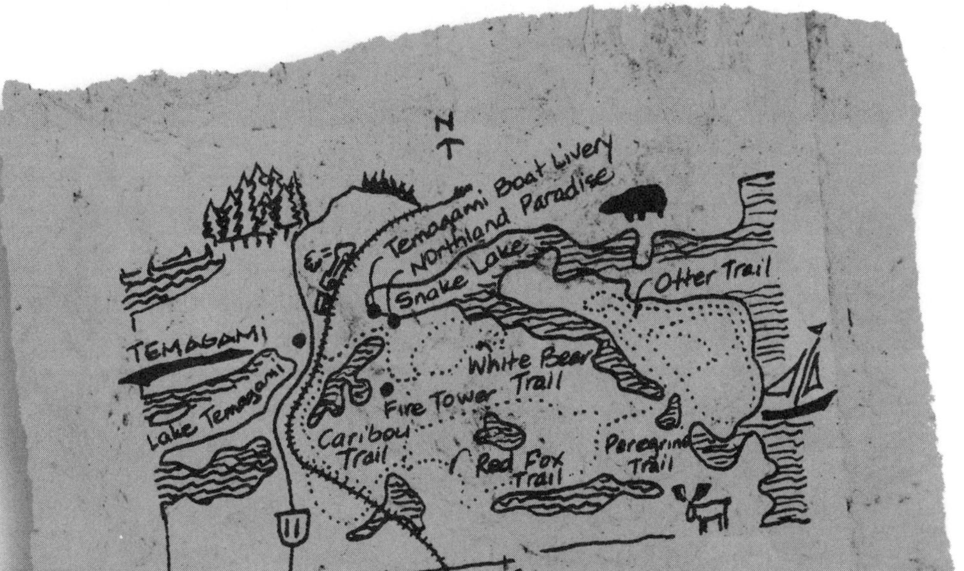

40 *Temagami White Bear Adventure*

It's all about facing your fears, hikers. I was feeling uneasy last Friday morning when I dropped the Three Babes off at Mine Bay at the end of the Lake Temagami Access Road. I watched sadly as they jumped into the Camp Wabikon launch, and the more-than-capable arms of teen heartthrob look-alike and camp owner's son Matthew. Mattman whisked the babes away across the big water, and left me standing there alone and waving goodbye. Here I was in Mother Nature's Paradise, Temagami, home of the White Bear Old Growth Forest, granite land of a thousand lakes, and I didn't have any idea what to do next. I had nothing planned. I was so bummed.

What do you do when you have time on your hands in a far-off place? Do you feel as uneasy as I do? To be honest with you, the instinct was to go home in the rain, drive the five hours back to Toronto and the relative security of hearth and home, instead of forging on down the lake and into the forest. There's something ominous and awesome, quiet and intimidating about the north of Ontario when it's only li'l old you and not much to do! This empty feeling always overtakes me on the road up north when I'm not moving towards an objective, like a hike or a meeting with friends. Thank goodness my rebellious inner voice struck out, and just in time too, as I was gassing up for the five-hour trip back to Toronto.

"What the hell's the matter with you, Kirby?" I quietly castigated myself. "The outdoor possibilities today are limitless! Just put one foot in front of the other and stop thinking so much! Just because it's cold and rainy doesn't mean you can't find adventure. Go get the boat at the marina and see what happens. Pull yourself together, chicken head!"

So I cleaned all the Tim's coffee and hot-chocolate cups and cinnamon-raisin bagel bags out of the car, regained some sense of Babeless order, and headed down to the Temagami Boat Livery to check on my big boat, *Nemesis*, whose engines have been running a little iffy lately, just the other side of trustworthy.

There's no feeling like that icy terror that comes down on you when you're 15 miles from either cottage or marina and the big Mercury baby starts coughing at you, begging you to do something. That's 100 horsepower of trouble.

On my way to the boat, I drove past the Northland Paradise Lodge, only to see my old pal Doug Adams, the best damned trapper, hiker, and wilderness guide this side of the Temiskaming River, out working on one of his aluminum-hulled Starcraft, so I yelled at him that it was time we hiked the White Bear together.

Dougie's the guy who blazed most of the White Bear's trails through the massive white and red pines just to the east of the fire tower. He owns that forest like it's his living room, so he'll teach me what I need to know about the White Bear, if I can just get him out there. To my joyful surprise, Doug says, "How 'bout tomorrow morning?"

Perfect! Now I'm not only staying in Temagami overnight, but I've also got a big-ass hike to look forward to. Hiker Mike can build an entire weekend agenda around that anchor hike. "Tomorrow morning at ten, Hiker Mike," says Trapper Doug. "And by the way, we're taking a dozen Boy Scouts from Burlington with us." Hey ho! That sure changes the tone of the hike now, don't it?

So what to do this afternoon and evening, I asked myself as I drove the few remaining yards to the Boat Livery. How about a boat ride, you simpleton, I shot back at myself, since we're here? The *Nemesis*, as it happens, was sitting dockside humming happily at a semi-high idle, as Terry the Inscrutable Boat Fixer tinkered and tuned. He's rude, he smokes far too much, and he grunts his answers at you. He has no use for summer interlopers from Big Smoke. Normally you'd move around a character like Terry, way around, but he's the only one who can make my damned engines sing, and he knows it, so I put up with his definitive lack of charm. His wife, Bonnie, on the other hand, is a great gal who'll go out of her way to help because she knows being nice to customers is good for business.

So I untied the beast, jumped into the cockpit, cranked the gas and thundered forward, straight the hell out of the harbour and down through the well-marked narrows at a reasonably high speed, hitting the big water of the White Bear, north of Flag Island, and shooting across the mirror and into the blue, surrounded on all green-forest sides by the Great Tree Spirit and all his pals.

Now I hadn't been up and across White Bear since 1973, when we all came to tent on top of the Big Rock Face of Red Pine Ridge year after year in the halcyon summers of our youth. Actors, singers, dancers and painters, all of a quarter century in age, all full of the joy of life, laughing and singing and making love around the fire at night, while jumping screaming, naked, from the heights of the Red Pine Ridge into the limitless blue-brown depths of the deep water close to shore — Temagami. Actors Jeff Braunstein; Maja Ardal; David and Sari Yorston, now of Perth, Australia; and artists Roger Griese and the late, great Don Phillips, would all bring their tents on the 24th of May, spend exceedingly long weekends through the season of serendip and pull up stakes and head for home on Thanksgiving if it hadn't already snowed by Labour Day.

Red Pine Ridge. I was going back and my feelings were mixed. Let me try to describe Red Pine Ridge. As you come eastward towards the end of Cassels Lake and the inlet leading to the pretty portage to Blueberry Lake, you will see a gigantic rock slash against the tree-line horizon, starting high up — 75 to 100 feet on its north end — and gradually slanting down to the water's edge on its south end, where amongst the wave-splashed boulders you'll find a natural U-shaped harbour of granite tucked in out of the wind, and a stump to tie up to. The ground is composed of smooth boulder, and a soft pine-needle pathway runs back up from the water through 1,000 massive red pines to a sheltered campsite and fireplace, complete with old logs for sitting and a rocky promontory high out into the lake for high diving and writing this piece. A natural rock pocket beckons like the hollow of God's hand. This cat-bird seat looks back down Cassels Lake from whence you came, so not only can you see anyone approaching for miles, you have the perfect westward sunset vista just before the stars come out, sharing the nighttime stage with the Aurora Borealis Dancers. You remember them from the old *Jackie Gleason Show*? As I sat there nestled in the rocks atop the diving place, my back to the fire and campsite, I marvelled at how soft the ground felt, covered of course with the red-pine needles and mossy loam of countless undisturbed years. The pines had grown since I was last here in 1973, as one would imagine, and they had increased their size considerably. This I know, because I remember the rocks to be higher off the water than they actually are, and the trees to be more modest — like a kid remembering an adult being much taller in the past.

It was the spring of 1971. I had just finished performing in Berthold Brecht's *A Man's a Man*, at the Bronfman Theatre in Montreal. The weather was wonderfully warm, and I was drawn to adventure after three months on stage. So instead of taking the boring old 401 back to Toronto and beginning the audition grind once again, I steered the rickety Vauxhall north and west up along the Ottawa River on Old Highway 17, towards North Bay.

Trapper, hiker, guide Doug Adams is short-tempered, intolerant, but totally endearing. Next day, chain smoking, he took us into the bottom of the White Bear Old Growth Forest, towards the 3,000-year-old portage trail the Aboriginal peoples used in order to avoid the heavy weather of Rabbit Lake. The trail moves south to north more or less, through a series of lakes called Flood and Pad (of lily fame) and Poison Pond (ivy), into the bottom of Peacours Bay on Snake Island Lake, about a mile of pristine back country (pine hills and cedar marsh), all the time following a good 2-foot-wide trail of moss and pine needles over the muskeg. The trail literally bounces up to say "Hi!" to your boots.

In one hour, I learned more about "Knowing Your Damned Trees" than I have in a lifetime. Did you know that balsam needles lie flat along the branches whereas white spruce needles grow around the branch, or that red-pine needles are 4 to 5 inches in length and grow in clumps of two, while white-pine needles are half as long and grow singly in a feathery light green sphere? You say you didn't know? Well, now you do, thanks to Doug Adams, who took us through Moose Pasture, where the great ones make their beds in the tall grasses close to their favourite food (the lily pads) and acid-water pools, where the moose mating battles are fought, the vegetable-salad suppers are celebrated, the loud, boisterous promises of love are made, and the little moose babies are created. We saw lots of bear prints in the lakeside mud, while a cormorant dove into the forest from above the river. I must tell you, hikers, that though I was a little miffed when Doug told me that a Boy Scout troop from Burlington were about to join us at the trail-head, after the intros were made and the hike started we all eased into friendly relations while moving through the 350-year-old pine giants towering over us. Doug identified every kind of herb and fern and moss and joe-pye flower — all the plants and animals native to the Old Growth Forest.

The trail back to the boat took less time, because Doug didn't stop every ten steps to show us something new. So we were able to boot it out real good for at least an hour. It started to rain on the way back to the boat; I'm convinced the rain was summoned by Doug's moose-call demonstration. Once back at Rainy and Lillian LaPerierre's guest cottage, I made a fire, stripped down to get warm, and ate Mars bars till dinner time, happy once again to be alive and kicking in the White Bear, close by Red Pine Ridge.

If you go to Temagami, take Highway 11 north past North Bay to Temagami. Stay with Rainy and Lillian LaPerierre at the Temagami Boat Livery, with cottages, canoes and boats for rent. Call 705-569-3321, or stay in the lodge with Hiker Doug Adams at Northland Paradise, with accommodation, all meals and guiding through the White Bear Old Growth Forest. Call 705-569-3791.

A little White Bear history. The Old Growth Ecosystem Forest is named for the White Bear family, Wabimakwa *in the Ojibwa language, whose historic and ancestral family hunting territory covered this particular area. The trails in the northern part were first developed by the White Bear family through the 3,000-year-old portage system that passes through the centre of the forest from Snake Island Lake to Cassels Lake. The provincial government has classified the White Bear as a conservation reserve. These areas have never been logged, mined or disturbed by the actions of man.*

41 *Hike Ontario: Working for Wilderness*

Each year, volunteers from across Ontario join teams of 12 people to help restore nature at outstanding natural areas in Ontario. Projects range from 2 to 15 days in length, and no experience is required. Projects this year include trail construction, improvements and restoration at Pelee Island, Bruce Trail in Grey County, Cedarcroft Trail near London, Maple Mountain Trail in Temagami and the Voyageur Trail in Lake Superior Provincial Park. Visit www.ontarionature.org or call 416-444-8419.

42 *Temagami Winter Hikes: The Christmas Fat Man Inside Me*

I bet you're all sitting around at home this morning wondering what on earth you're going to do over the Christmas Break. We tend to look at the upcoming holiday season with a little dread, knowing the amount of caloric intake that will be visited upon us in the form of dining and drinking pleasures. I can say personally that when it came time to pull the official wedding and funeral suit out of the back of the closet and get it all fixed up and cleaned for the round of upcoming parties, the pants were just a little too snug around the middle, and the parties have only just begun. The Fat Man Inside Me screaming to get out is finding an escape hatch. Time to up the physical activity once again. So, hikers and outdoor people, what can we do to balance the books?

Here's a holiday activity. Doug just called me from the Northland Paradise Lodge in Temagami to give me the rundown on the Christmas Break activities in Temagami's winter wonderland. It's Big Snow Country, folks. Temagami is the non-consumptive eco-tourism capital of Canada. You can stay at the Northland Paradise Lodge for $75 per person per night, including three full meals per day and loads of outdoor fun. The lodge is right on the lake just to the north of the White

Bear Old Growth Forest, and Hiker Doug will guide you along a 3,000-year-old trapline on foot or on snowmobile. You can even go ice-fishing for pickerel and trout in warm and cozy ice-fishing huts out on the lake. Doug will also take you snowshoeing through the White Bear Forest, and if you haven't tried dogsledding across the frozen tundra, now's your chance.

Temagami is a $4\frac{1}{2}$-hour drive through Northern Ontario from downtown Toronto and is a great place for a family outing or a romantic rendezvous, and with kids paying half price, it won't kill your wallet.

Contact Doug Adams at 705-569-3791 or on the Web at paradise@onlink.net.on. Doug's wife makes wonderful, guilt-free, low-calorie meals, and all that outdoor activity will melt the Fat Man right off your middle.

43 *Paddle Your Own Damn Canoe!*

I have an old cedar cottage down at the bottom of Rabbit Lake in Temagami, and just three cottages away from me live two of Canada's most celebrated canoeists and outdoors people — Gary and Joanie McGuffin from London, Ontario.

Gary and Joanie first sprang to national prominence when, in 1987, they recorded their remarkable canoe odyssey across Canada by water in their first book, *Where Rivers Run*. To fulfill their dream of travelling from sea to sea in a canoe, the recently married couple set out from the Gulf of St. Lawrence. Two years, 6,000 miles and 10-million paddle strokes later, they reached the open waters of the Beaufort Sea. Challenging many of the country's most dangerous rivers, the McGuffins realized a dream and discovered a Canada that few of us will ever see. Now, years later, the McGuffins have written the most compelling, comprehensive and enlightening canoeing techniques book on this planet.

Paddle Your Own Canoe sets a new standard for "how to" books. Ten years in the making, *Paddle Your Own Canoe* is designed for both the beginner and the seasoned canoeist, with expert instruction in canoeing philosophy, fitness and balance,

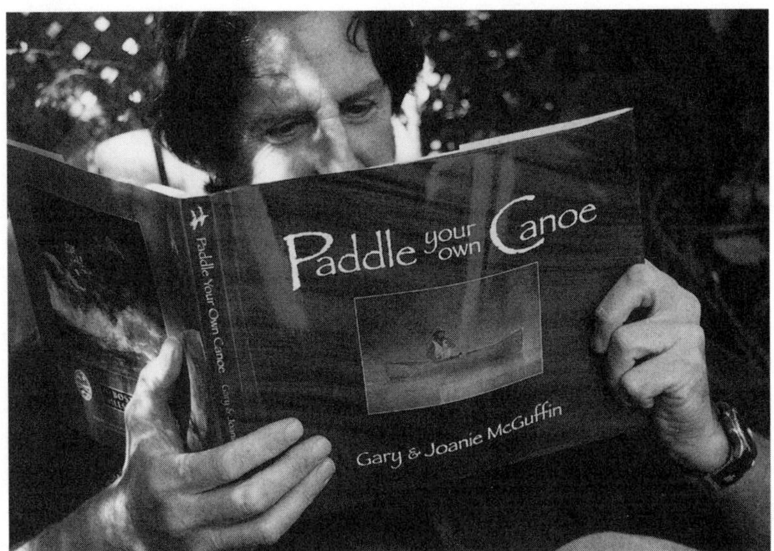

reading the river, advanced turns and manoeuvres — even how to tie a canoe onto your vehicle properly.

The book is written in a clear, friendly and accessible style and contains everything you need to know to start right into the sport of canoeing. Good on ya, Gary and Joanie McGuffin! *Paddle Your Own Canoe* is published by Boston Mills Press and can be purchased at any reputable bookstore. Hiker Mikey likes it, and so will you.

ADIRONDACK RV TREKS

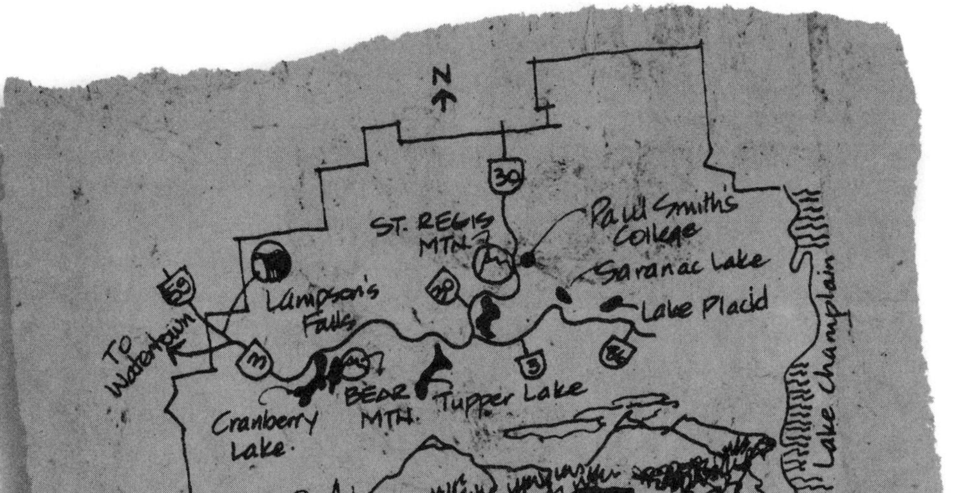

44 *The Game is Afoot*

Tracker Dave and I share the same fantasy: load up a bunch of hiking gear, sound equipment, coupla guitars and smelly dog Rupert, and head out in a big camper van along the old north shore of Lake Ontario and turn south at Kingston into the Adirondack Mountains. And that little dream of ours took a sharp right turn towards reality this morning. Dave Sammut from Bolton's Motor Home Vacations Canada called me with a great idea. Dave rents out hundreds of RVs during the busy summertime camping season, but suggested we take one of his 22-foot Classic Royal Expeditions for a good long ride after Thanksgiving, when things slow down a bit. I thanked Dave for his suggestion and then made mention of my present conundrum. Boston Mills had me under contract for a new Hiker Mike book called *Farther Afield*, due out next spring, and I would have to take the Adirondack Adventure this summer in order to meet my fall deadline. Dave gave my problem some thought, and after checking his August reservations, found a cancellation the weekend of August 16–18. "Would that do?"

My dad and mom took little Hiker Mikey and his three brothers, Sean, Dan and Chris, to the Adirondacks for a camping trip in 1957. We jammed up the Packard with sleeping bags, pillows, coolers, Coleman stove and lantern and lived in two tents for a month across upstate New York, Vermont, New Hampshire and Massachusetts, as far east and south as Cape Cod. But the lifetime highlight, the heart-thumping, chub-inducing, pre-teen bittersweet memory of Adirondack National Park blows all the other kid reminiscences out of the water. And water is what I remember most. The misty greens of Fish Creek Pond, Tupper and Saranac Lakes — not to mention Lake Placid, home of the Winter Olympics — all live within me still!

Cool, fragrant, cedar-lined shores enveloped multi-coloured, flat, smooth stone beaches, while frogs and ducks watched me fishing for perch in the shallows. I first discovered girls in the Adirondack Mountains. Sandy Matson, with the white-blond halo, wore a tight, sky-blue Speedo just like me. We swam together in the dusk and held each other's hand while walking the gladed path through the bush to the variety store, almost kissing but not quite sure how to begin or what to do with our bodies. (The technique was to be honed later after more dance practice at the Catholic Youth mixers of my early teens.) Sandy Matson lived in Fairhaven, New York, and wrote to me for a while. She was my first pure love — all heart and soul — and that's how I remember the Adirondacks. So I hope I'm not setting myself up for a large disenchantment upon my arrival in a potential American Shopping Mall State Park complete with McDonald's Mountain Burgers and Six Flags Over Saratoga. But Yes to Everything, hikers. We'll play it as it lays.

Dave the Tracker Man, my folkie singer-songwriter pal, will be just finishing up his new album, entitled *Get Me the Hell Outta Here*, and so I will load up the Trailhead Express with all the gear and pull Dave out of the sound studio to begin the quest to return to our youth and the halcyon hiking days of childhood yesteryear.

I didn't think this plan would ever play itself out. After I had originally mentioned my Adirondack stratagem to my morning-show host and pal John Donabie, he suggested I call Ron Hewitt, former voice of the Toronto Maple Leafs and erstwhile sales guru at CFRB. Ron had a question for me. "Who the hell is gonna give you a free Winnie in the middle of high season? Let me check my sources at Budget and I'll get back to you." If you've ever waited for Ronasonic to get back to you, you know that a lot of time can pass, and since I'm closing in on yet another birthday, I just don't have it. The time, that is! So I turned away from commercial radio and struck out to find my forest friends, those runners of the north Toronto woods, the hiking congregation.

And it just so happened that I had been up Bolton way not two weeks before, hiking on the world-famous Humber Valley Heritage Trail, when I noticed a ton of RV rental companies lining the highway leading into sleepy little Bolton town. This past spring I had given my Everest Base Camp slide show at the HVHT's Annual General Meeting. After the show, my long-time hiking friend Dan O'Reilly had told me that, in lieu of payment, if there was anything he could ever do to further the Hiker Mike cause etc. . . . So I called in the marker. "Dan, old buddy, who do you know in the RV biz who may be able to spring for a camper van to take to the mountains for a weekend? And after Dan took the pleasure of asking me, "Who the hell is gonna cough up a camper in high season?" he most graciously gave me Dave Sammut's phone number. And the rest is history, about to be made. Friends in high places? Fie! It's not who you know, gentle pilgrim, it's who you hike with! The cost for the RV Classic Royal, three double beds, shower, kitchen, microwave, TV and Blaupunkt sound system, is $1,600 per week, which is being donated to the project in return for a million bucks worth of publicity on land, on sea, and radio, because I'm telling you right now, I'll never stop talking about my opportunity to come full circle with myself on the Adirondack Journey Back to Me. Thank you, Dave Sammut of Bolton, my new friend for life!

And now you know where to rent your recreational vehicle, hikers. Motor Home Vacations Canada, 12465 Highway 50, Bolton, ON, the largest retailer of motor homes, RVs and camper vans in our country. You can reach them at 1-800-672-3572.

45 *The Adirondack Adventure Begins*

I locked my door and the sun went down
I said Goodbye to Boston town
Mass Turnpike and Route 15
S'gonna take me on down
To the New York scene.
'I'm on the road again.'
— Tom Rush, circa 1965

Dave and I drove up to Motorhome Vacations Canada, where our host was waiting with our 22-foot Classic Royal Expedition. We were shown how everything works, from the electronics and the propane, the fridge and the stove, to the toilet and the television. Tracker Dave and I spent a half an hour transferring our gear from the car to the camper, and after stowing the stuff and making all secure, we fired it up and ever so gingerly edged out of the lot and into the traffic. We were blatantly buffeted from side to side by giant tractor trailers and Greyhound buses that made it their business to bully us over into the old-fart lane in a big, fat, scary hurry. And this lane is where we lived for the rest of our journey to Gananoque. We met our third hiker buddy, Stormy Blake Stormes, my oldest and bestest friend, at the corner of Highway 9 and Highway 50. At last, the Three Hiketeers were on their way to the Magical Mountain Kingdom of Adirondack.

The RV's recommended speed is 80 to 90 kph, so it didn't take us long to settle into the six-hour highway journey. Tracker Dave took over the wheel while Stormy rode shotgun in the big cushy captain's chairs up front. I found the dining table's bench a most comfortable perch from which to write my thoughts and enjoy the sunny, passing early evening scene coming at me from the wide cinerama windows on every side: the green and golden forest fields of the northern shore of Lake Ontario and the deep blue razor slash of watery horizon to our southern right, while the fat, pink and hazy old sun sank into the pollution of Big Smoke Toronto in the rear-view window.

Past Gananoque, we turned south onto the 1,000 Islands Parkway, which soon delivered us up to the KOA (Kampgrounds of America) under a million stars nestled nicely between Ivy Lea and the bridge to America, which we saved until the next day. That first night, we found a camping site with electric hookup, so we plugged in, lit up the wagon, and took our tokes for a long, dark walk back down the road. The KOA smelled of swimming-pool chlorine and musty tent canvas, which always shoots me, straight and happy, back to childhood. Mom and Dad used to pull out those old 'n' moldy army tents and make us live in them for a couple of weeks each summer. That canvas smell reminds me of my first kiss and my wiener getting caught in my blue jeans zipper — two entirely separate incidents, by the way — and a thousand other ecstasies and agonies that inhabit the back side of my memory bank.

I was getting undressed inside my sleeping bag on a rainy night. It took both my parents and the couple in the tent next door to extricate my wiener from the zipper, in what must have been the most agonizingly embarrassing evening of my time spent here on earth. I have used the zipper-and-the-wiener scenario for many of my emotional recollections while doing scene study in acting class. And my first kiss? We'll get to that later.

Of all the soundless stars hanging just over our Ivy Lea heads, the Big Dipper and the North Star were most prevalent; Canadian stars. Ironic, being so close to the American border. The next day, Interstate 81 would take us south to Watertown and the Adirondack Mountains beyond.

The 1,000 Islands area is a natural bridge for the migration of animals from the Algonquin Land Dome southward over the waters of the Frontenac Axis to the Adirondack Dome. Now there's a trail that lets hikers and bikers travel this ancient granite ridge used for millennia by man and beast. The Algonquin to Adirondack International Trail (A2A) is located on secondary county roads and unmaintained road allowances, offering spectacular scenery and an up-close look at Eastern Ontario's rural communities. For more info call The Watershed, at 27 King Street East in Gananoque, Ontario, K7G 1E8. The number is 613-382-4989, and they'll send you a brochure and map.

You could spend half a lifetime hiking from Algonquin Park down the Frontenac Axis to the Adirondacks. These trails, like the Trans Canada, are more a grand ideal than a reality for modern man. Wouldn't it be lovely to have the time to walk the big ones? Mecca? Jerusalem? Camino de Santiago? The Quest for the Holy Trail? There's a book in there somewhere.

This KOA was my first, and now I can understand what makes these overnight oases such a popular draw with RVs. We pulled up to the closed office at 10 PM and signed in on our own, found a campsite with electric hook-up quite easily, went for a quiet walk under the sparkling celestial canopy, played some guitar music well into the night, fell asleep amidst the quiet forest peace and woke refreshed with the dawn. KOA bathrooms are clean, the ambiance is comfortable,

and the people we met were most friendly and accommodating. KOA is as predictable as a McDonald's or a Best Western, which makes for a good night's sleep. I'm going back.

46 *Lampson's Falls*

We slipped quietly out of the campground around 7:30 AM, heading over the 1,000 Island Bridge into New York State and clearing customs without incident — no intrusive beagle dogs sniffing our backpacks in the RV, just a few occupational questions and we were on our way heading south to Watertown, N.Y., on Interstate 81, a grand and winding way into the American heartland. Highway 3, a more modest two-lane blacktop, took us east through the guts of the thriving city of Watertown, but it wasn't until we passed Carthage that we began to realize that the hills were starting to steepen, and the bush began to thicken deciduously. We were entering the foothills of the mighty Adirondack Mountains.

Highway 3 is a wide, black ribbon of highway, well-marked, accommodating our wheelhouse with its gracious curves and rises, and I was feeling like Jackson Browne heading down the good road on the bus looking for the next adventure, with Elton John singing "Goodbye Norma Jean" on the radio. I didn't know if I would be able to write longhand on the fly, sitting at the dinette table, but the scribbling turned out just this side of readable, and my cushy seat afforded me a view out the front windshield. So I could check out the oncoming log cabins, maple-syrup signs and wood-carved, life-sized Indian chiefs and black bears in front of all the souvenir shops we passed. Here it was mid-August, a good month after the 4th of July holiday, and everybody was still flying the American flag in front of their houses. I love Americans — they put their feelings out front. What you see is what it is.

When we arrived at the pretty little town of Fine, we turned north onto County Road 77 and headed for de Grasse. Once there, we continued north on what is now called Clare Road, and less than 5 miles later came upon the entrance to the Grasse

River Wild Forest, the home of Adirondack Hike Number 1 — Lampson's Falls and the mighty Grasse River.

Lampson's Falls is a 30-foot waterfall chute at 45 degrees, and halfway down the wall is a natural 8-foot bathtub cut into the rock, with a freshwater feed from the falls above and overflow drainage, keeping the captured water cool and fresh. A perfect spot to get naked, read a book and enjoy your favourite Cuban cigar — Hiker Heaven under the afternoon sun. You can follow the wall down to a sandy beach, complete with a round log-circle campfire, all sheltered by two giant granite rocks thrusting breast-like proudly out into the pond. Camp here if you can, hikers. It's only ten minutes walk from the main gates and your car. Although the falls are loud and boisterous, the sound soon blends into the quiet of the wind and rustling leaves.

After Lampson's Falls, we followed a series of rapids, cataracts, little falls and chutes leading northward into ever-deepening, ferrous-tinged stone pools. At the beginning of the hike, the path is over 4 feet wide and most gentle, covered with tree roots, pine cones, and red needles. The trail stays halfway between the valley walls and floor, so the ups and

downs are minimal. You'll find many paths to follow, but for the best results keep closer to the river with the morning sun on your back.

The further up the river trail you go, the more the forest begins to close in on you. Wild raspberries and sharp nettles attempt to mar your way, along with fallen trees; it's apparent that no attempt has been made to maintain the trail by restoring the rotting corduroy roads, steps and railings. But that's half the charm, if you enjoy the challenge of following a disappearing trail. And never fear, the N.Y. State Forest Rangers have, at some time in the distant past, nailed up little faded red plastic circles onto the flanks of the old-growth trees with big, fat nails.

About 45 minutes downriver, we came to an old broken-down log chute that used to cross the raging torrent, but no longer. This bridge was to have been our jump-over point to join up with the yellow-marked trail, which used to run up and down the west side of the mighty Grasse River. Since we couldn't get across, we continued to move downriver on the east side, into the wilderness, and our riverside pathway eventually disappeared, while we still had no luck finding a crossing. So we turned around after an hour and backtracked, attempting to locate our red trail once again. We found it finally, back at the old washed-out bridge, so we knew for certain that this was where we were meant to cross to the yellow trail.

But who cares really? This Lampson's Falls river walk was only a warm-up for the rest of the weekend, and we're not lost as long as we can hear the river. And since the Sherpas are never the ones to take the wussy way out, we stripped naked at the washed-out bridge, threw our clothes and boots into our backpacks and successfully completed a most precarious crossing of the rushing water.

Re-robing on the far shore, we headed up the old, unused logging road in search of yellow markers, and although we found a few old and faded, Mother Nature had re-taken control of the trail and turned it into thick and impenetrable bush once again. Retracing our newly made trail back to the bridge, we decided that this was the best spot for lunch, a swim and a respite, before crossing back to the east side and heading upriver to our camper and calling it a day.

We picked up some groceries and beer in Tupper Lake and headed north on Highway 30 to the home of my youthful dreams, rife with those sweet, aching reminiscences that still haunt me today: Fish Creek Pond, where we'll stay tonight, and hike St. Regis Mountain Friday.

47 *Fish Creek Pond*

Fish Creek Pond, the idealized campsite of my youth, lives in vernal splendour in the Adirondack Forest Preserve on Route 30, just 12 miles north of Tupper Lake, New York.

Fish Creek is a sandy-bottomed, shallow lake full of perch, surrounded by old-growth red and white pine. The well-maintained campsites are flat and sandy. Most of them are 40 to 50 feet wide by 100 feet deep and lead you down to the pond and your own private beach. Campers bring their canoes and watercraft with them to play in the shallows. The lake is 4 miles around, and every inch of shoreline is campsite, while across the road and in the bush live the many hiking trails, wash and shower rooms, and activity venues for volleyball, theatre, countless activities for kids and adults, and a most beautiful and holy Chapel in the Pines for worship.

The Otter Hollow loop and the Floodland loop connect at a big footbridge over Fish Creek to form an 8.5-mile track through beautiful forest. The Smokies (that's Yank for Forest Rangers) do recommend you take a topographical map, compass, whistle, water, proper clothing and footwear, because a mile in the deep woods is much longer than you might think if you're not properly prepped.

Next time we come, I'm bringing lovely Libby and the Three Babes for an extended stay in a motorhome vacation RV. Fish Creek Pond is still the most beautiful of Adirondack Campgrounds, and with all sites directly on the shoreline and access to Saranac Lake, it is very popular with boaters.

How to get to Fish Creek? Take 401 east past Kingston, south on the 1,000 Islands Parkway to Interstate 81 and Watertown, N.Y., east into the mountains on N.Y. Route 3, and north on Route 30 to Tupper Lake and Fish Creek Pond.

48 *Mount St. Regis*

What a truly amazing four-hour hike! Mount Regis reigns! Imagine, if you will, a 3,000-foot, forested Vesuvian cone of a mountain jutting proudly out of a bowl of salad greens 50 miles across, surrounded by lowland lakes and lesser rolling foothills, the lands at her base stretching out to a ring of the highest Adirondack Mountains rimming the horizon. Standing atop the rounded, bald granite dome of St. Regis Mountain, next to the abandoned fire tower, I could see in every direction the high peaks of Whiteface and Mackenzie Mountains and the million lakes, including Tupper, Saranac and Fish Creek Ponds, all the way east to Lake Placid. There was so much panorama atop Mount St. Regis we just stood there slack-jawed, slowly turning clockwise, quietly whispering expletives of astonishment under our breaths.

The summit is not easily won. Although the pathway is wide and welcoming, and the first hour is lightly uphill, the trail takes a distinctly nasty vertical bent for the next arduous hour. You'll know you're in for some serious ups after you've stopped

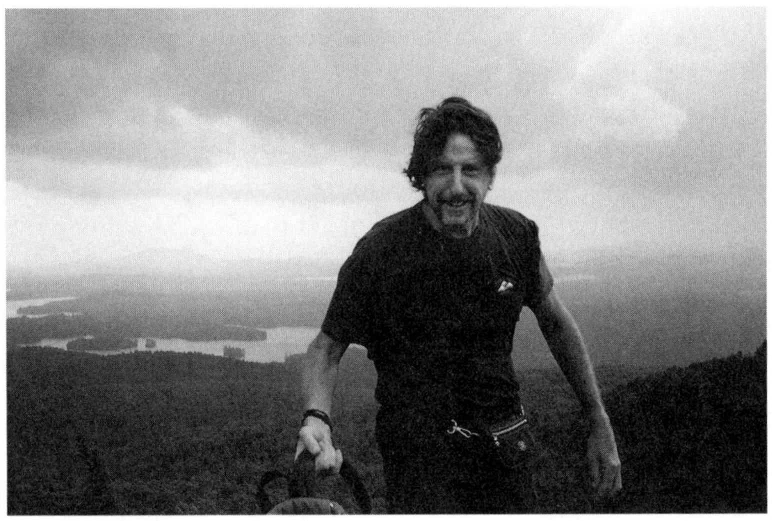

for your water break at the picnic area (with outhouse) just past the little stream. Then the trail heads up a bunch of newly built stairs of wood, and that's the last time you'll breathe easy until achieving the summit. The last third of the hike seems relentless, and just as you start to quietly question your abilities, you'll see the sky appear through the foliage and you'll know you're not far. But the true humiliation happens when a bunch of Paul Smith's College kids run up the trail past your tired, broken body just under the summit. These kids from the college work on trail maintenance and restoration as part of their degree, and it shows.

I had been soaking wet with sweat when I finally hit the top, but Old Mother West Wind dried me off in minutes. After sharing a lunch of Cambozola, and nectarines, and indulging in some bud, we headed delightfully down that two-hour-long trail back to our camper, pacing ourselves somewhere between a lollygag and a meander.

The distance from the Route 30 parking lot to the summit of St. Regis and back is 6 miles, with a vertical rise of 1,235 feet. The boot took us better than four hours with a lunch break. Directions are simple: from Watertown, take Highway 3 east to Tupper Lake. Turn north on Highway 30 past Paul Smith's Town, and 7 miles beyond Lake Clear junction turn left off 30 onto Keese Mills Road. Head west past the college 2½ miles, and look for the St. Regis Mountain parking lot on the left. St. Regis Mountain will give you Big View in spades and you'll return to your campsite or lodge with a tremendous feeling of well being. You'll also want to sit still for a few hours. Five-star, four-hour. Magnifico!

49 *Fish Creek and Rollins Pond Wilderness Circle*

For our last hike, we chose to stay within the confines of the state park, utilizing their excellent system of beautifully manicured hiking and canoe portage trails which, as mentioned earlier, formed a delightful foray into deep wilderness. Hard, wide, red-dirt trails and the occasional bike and walking gravel paths lie just inside the bush from the road, which passes the hundreds of waterfront campsites. From the top of Rollins Pond we made it out past the main gates for lunch at the Owl's Nest in just under three hours, took an hour for R and R, then headed back into Fish Creek Pond for the return run. About an hour into the re-trek, we had stopped to sit on a stump for a water break, when a Smokie pulled up in his Jeep and arrested us, not for loitering in a state park, but for failing to surrender our campsite by 11 AM, the time now being 2:30 PM. Instead of throwing us into the hoosegow, he proceeded to drive us back to the campsite, where we quickly removed the offending RV, under the harsh glare of the outdoor family who had been waiting for what must have seemed an eternity to set up their tents and begin their camping holiday.

Fish Creek Pond is a little piece of hiking Nirvana tucked away in the giant red-pine forest next to the shores of Saranac Lake. The park ecology is healthy: the chipmunks are fat in the forest and the frogs are plentiful in the ponds — always a good sign when amphibians are thriving. The campsites are large and clean, as campers are responsible for their own garbage; only recyclables are collected — refuse must leave with the campers. The trails accommodate lots of hikers and take them past pristine forest lakes and rivers that normally only a canoeist would see. The bathrooms are across the road in the bush, and the lights are activated by motion sensors for energy conservation.

Fish Creek Pond is also a great place to bring the kids, not just for the beach swimming and boat rentals but for the full board of activities presented daily, including volleyball, tie-dying, crafts, bird and butterfly shows, blues concerts, and live theatre. There is also Sunday church service in an exquisite setting — a cathedral surrounded by giant red pine, and acoustically very sound for folk singing, as my friend Tracker David Bradstreet so elegantly demonstrated when he stood up on the altar and sang his signature hit, "Renaissance."

Some 40-odd years had come and gone since I had camped at Fish Creek Pond, but it seemed like only a season or two had passed since I had last seen my summer friend. A tear came to my eye when Tracker Dave sang the words, "Let's dance that old dance once more." The little boy still lives within.

Pen Pal: Mike — Head Way West, Young Hiker

"Hey, Mike: We're hiking the West Coast Trail this August and we're seeking out the toughest, hilliest trails in our area to train on (up to and around a one-hour radius of Etobicoke). Do you know of any good cardio workers? We've been doing the Hockley Valley Side Trails and the Waterdown to Dundas trail with our full packs, so far they've been the best. If you know of anything more physically challenging, by all means let us know!"

— *Mike Petersen, Etobicoke, Ontario*

"Funny you should mention the west coast. Kayak Mike Allison and I are just on our way to hike the wilds of Vancouver and Whistler, and these are the Megacity hiking trails on which I've been training. You looking for a killer boot? How about the Credit Valley Footpath — up and down the steep, slippery side of the valley walls. Or how about the Humber Valley Trail from Palgrave to Bolton — three full hours of cardiovascular." — *HM*

VANCOUVER TO WHISTLER: The B.C. Blitz

I have been both blessed and cursed with a tricky lower back, a condition I can trace to that raucous summer of '78 at Camp White Pine in Haliburton, where an unruly group of young actors lived outdoors and slept on the ground all night in the foggy dew while shooting a picture called *Meatballs*. You can still catch Hiker Mike limping around in this sophomoric blockbuster movie, trying to corral the baby campers, doped to the gills on Percodan, grinning stupidly ear to ear. Nowadays, I am allowed rigorous exercise only with the proper warm-up, but every so often I'll get that familiar electric shock down next to my coccyx when I make an unsupported move, and that's my warning to slow down and relax or else my back will go out completely and I will have to lie down on the sidelines for at least three days. (It happened in Nassau, Bahamas, last winter while hiking the Exuma chain.)

And so it was, the night before I was to leave on the B.C. Blitz (the Nootka Five-day Wilderness Hike). I loaded up my backpack — clothes, books, food, utensils for cooking, sleeping bag and Thermorest etc., buckled the chest and shoulder straps, and was about to close the waist buckles when *zap*, like a bolt of lightning right up my ass, I got the warning from Mt. Olympus: "Put down the bag, you moron, your backpacking days are over."

This new development not only was unfortunate, as all plans to fly in to the Nootka Trail on the northwest coast of Vancouver Island had already been made, but embarrassing as well. I had already announced to the world on my weekend hiking show that we were leaving the next day for Nootka. My 25-year-old nephew, Kayak Mike Allison, was out in B.C. all packed and waiting for me, ready to hit this wild rainforest trail along the Pacific shoreline. But I've finally reached an age where I can see the wall writing, so here's what I did.

First, I turned the backpack bag upside down, dumped out the overnight stuff, took only my shorts and t-shirt, three pairs of socks, my Gore-Tex rain shell and a book and grabbed my LoweAlpine Vision 40 backpack and filled it halfway. Wow. I just moved down the weigh scale from 45 pounds to 10 pounds! Wicked and totally manageable. Now I can walk on board the plane wearing what I'll be hiking in — New Balance Storm Cloud 7 light and flexible boots, MEC nylon river pants, a LoweAlpine multi-purpose nylon long-sleeved shirt, and my 10-pound walk-on backpack. Next up, I called the Big Blonde Kayak Boy and broke the bad news about nixing the Nootka backpacking trip, suggesting instead that we do a series of day hikes carrying nothing but water. I expected a blast of supreme disappointment from my adventure sidekick. Instead the phone filled up with, "Awesome, compadre. Now we can hike all the best trails out here and see the whole damned country." That's why I love hiking with Kayak Mike. No matter what goes down, it's always the right thing.

I arrived at the Vancouver terminal to discover Kayak Mike, my mountain consort, waiting for me at the luggage carousel and my cell phone ringing in my pocket with a call from the residents of the House of Women back in Toronto. Mother and the Merry Little Breezes had me on the speaker back in the common room desiring collectively to know whether or not I had arrived safely.

Kayak Boy scooped up the phone as I wrestled my Vision 40 backpack from the carousel, and we headed south through the sunny, bright terminal and down the big stairs to the bald Budget Rent-A-Car guy with a small furry animal perched on his pate, just above his forehead. I was so close to asking him if it was beaver or martin. Whatever the species, I swear his rug was on sideways, but Mr. Budget made it very easy to jump into a bright-yellow Mustang convertible, and moments later we came out of the tunnel and into the mind-blasting vision that is the giant green conifer cover of the Coast Mountains, rising up out of the silver-blue and sparkling Pacific, filled to the brim with a million islands and tankers and horizons.

The vision rises into motion for me — strong excitement, danger, adventure. I want to dive into the picture, crawl inside the big mountain-ocean movie and co-star with it for a full week of heavy hiking, topped up with a great hotel, a hot tub and the best night's sleep. So this is the plan: Yes to Everything! The only agenda? Every day we do a scream-for-mercy, I'm-gonna-die, I've-finally-gone-too-far hike.

So we got off the plane and headed directly to Grouse Mountain and the home of the Herculean Vertical Hike — the Grouse Grind.

50 *The Grouse Grind: Vancouver*

The sign at the base of the Grind told me the record time to summit is 24 minutes, so I drew an optimistic breath into my unopened lungs and stepped into the steep staircase of tree roots and jagged rock. I was about to experience the toughest "up" this side of Namche Bazaar. After an hour or so of climbing up impassable 2-foot risers on the ladder from hell, just as I was about to puke up my guts and die, I heard the hum of the gondola through the old-growth cedar and fir, and I was certain the summit could not be far beyond. It was then that I arrived at the wooden poster nailed to a tree signifying the halfway mark! I was nauseous and disoriented by this point, grasping for the handrail and missing, so I took every opportunity to step off the trail at switchbacks, pretending to be taking notes. Welcome to the West, Wussy Toronto Boy!

The Grouse Grind has no mercy, and no escape, and it's too dark by this time to turn around and go back down. At the three-quarter point, we swung around to the western sunset view, and the rest of the grind up to the restaurant and gondola was slowly and painfully accomplished. We took an hour and 40 minutes and left a lot of first-timer sweat on the trail, which we replaced with great bottles of cold, sparkling water in the mountain-top café, then enjoyed the sun setting over Vancouver Island while riding the gondola down into the darkness, to our canary-yellow convertible far below.

51 *The Cypress Bowl and Lord Baden Powell Trail*

For those of you who have never been to the west coast, you must imagine a series of high coastal mountains running north and south, covered with every kind of conifer, and moving quite abruptly down from the sky to the sea. One is never far away from the many ski trails, Grouse Mountain and the Cypress Bowl being the closest to town. Since Day 1 was somewhat recklessly begun with the Grouse Grind Trek, it only seemed fair to take on the mammoth Cypress Bowl and the Lord Baden Powell Trail on Day 2.

The trail that runs from Deep Cove in North Vancouver past the Second Narrows Bridge all the way, 42K to Horseshoe Bay in West Vancouver, is the Lord Baden Powell Trail. We had crossed it at Grouse yesterday and we began our hike up Cypress on this very same Baden Powell Trail today. And as we started heading skyward, we felt the ocean wind pick up from behind, giving us an encouraging pat on the butt and lending us a friendly hand on our way up a 15-foot-wide mix of sand-and-rock gravel trail on a 25-to-30-foot angle, as the sounds of the city began to disappear into the ocean mists below.

Every west coast trail seems to begin with an hour or three of Straight Up! B.C. hikers know you gotta pay big time before you play. First the big "ups," then the hike along the crest with the rewarding vista, then the long and agonizing

knee-wrenching "downs," in which new leg muscles are discovered and tortured individually, from the quads to the calves and the knees and all your painful little toes, which scream at you to stop: "Desist descending!"

An hour and a half later we came to a giant humpback granite rock atop Cypress, and a vista that defies any IMAX movie. Cypress Mountain looks down on teeny little quarter-mile-long, ocean-going freighters, anchored way far below in blue Burrard Inlet. Your unbelieving eyes follow the silver line of foothills on Vancouver Island, running hundreds of kilometres to Victoria in the south, and north to Johnston Strait, tucked under the snow-capped crest of the Comox Glacier. To the south we're given chase by hundreds of Coastal Mountains, coming up at us from Washington State. From the rocky top of Cypress, we look down on Horseshoe Bay and Howe Sound, leading east, deep into the Squamish forests, where "The Chief," the rock-faced giant, rules from on high. Directly across from us, Douglas firs point the way to "The Lions," twin rocky humps, weather-rounded and craggy gatekeepers through which snow-topped Mt. Garibaldi smiles back at us from up Whistler way.

The Cypress Trek was good for Day 2. Although we went high, it was by way of a series of meandering switchbacks across the flanks of the mountain. My cardiovascular factory was definitely open for business, but I hit the golden groove three quarters of the way up and truly enjoyed the climb. Let's say 2 hours and 20 minutes to the top.

"Mountain is wicked," shouts Kayak Mike. "The Coastals rule!" states this tall, thin blonde Viking stud of a youth, having lived 25 summers, most of which have been spent in the company of oceans, mountains, forests and glaciers. Michael whale watches and guides the big ocean kayaks up the Johnston Strait and into the Queen Charlottes in summer, and guides trekkers up the Franz Joseph Glacier on New Zealand's South Island in winter. This lean, golden sinew of a man has learned more about nature and the outdoors in his quarter century on the Big Ball than most of us know collectively. Mike's forest expertise is matched only by his boundless energy, unbridled optimism and infectious enthusiasm, but I do secretly believe the young bastard is trying to kill me with all these goddamn verticals.

After finishing that wonderful Cypress Bowl hike straight up to the top of the Coast Mountains and the Vancouver skyline, we jumped into the Mustang, put down the top to let in the sunlight, made one stop for jugs of water and headed out Highway 1 past Horseshoe Bay. We then turned our sights north on Highway 99, sailing up the Sea to Sky Highway into the misty blue, black and green mountains towards Squamish and our next destination — Whistler.

We followed the Sea to Sky with the long and deep Howe Sound on our left and that mountainous wall of conifer green on our right, until we crested a hill and the little town of Squamish sprang into view. "Big Chief," shouts Kayak Mike. "Rock climbers' heaven!" And that's when I saw it. The most massive granite rock-face monolith, striding a mile straight up into the blue, and just as wide. A wall of gunmetal grey, slashed with striated cuts, crevasses, ridges and climbing routes with names like Angels Crest, Apron up the Buttress, and Suicide, that'll bring primal shivers to anyone who imagines themself actually trying to climb The Chief. Perhaps the next lifetime for me. When you're 55 years old there are some adventures, one must admit, that are somewhat beyond one's capability. The Chief climb must wait for the next go-round.

Whistler Village is another hour up the Sea to Sky Highway from Squamish, and we arrived late in the sunny afternoon with the key to one of Whistler's original 40-year-old ski chalets, built by Vancouver businessman Jim Tutton, dear pal and old schoolmate of Urban Sherpa and two-time Genie-Award-winning actress Linda Sorensen. Jim splits his time, in Whistler on weekends and workweeks in West Vancouver, but also has another chalet in Sun City, Idaho. This guy knows his way around a ski mountain, so much so that visiting dignitaries to Whistler seek him out to guide them on their ski adventures. One such celebrity was none other than our late Prime Minister, Pierre Elliot Trudeau, who skied and partied with Jim for a week back in 1990.

Jim's directions to his B.C. cedar A-frame chalet were easy to follow, the key fit the lock like a hot knife in butter, and it wasn't an hour before we sat down to salmon steaks and broccoli at the great, long dining table, while the CBC brought us up to date on the Sydney Olympics. After dinner, we flung open the giant sliding-glass doors, stepped out onto the balcony and looked upon the mighty Whistler and Blackcombe Mountains, with the sparkling little alpine village of Whistler Creek at our feet. The sky dome over our heads was black as pitch, except for the stars and planets, which were as big and shiny as brass door knobs. I was so excited to be here in Whistler that I couldn't sleep for hours, which did not serve me well the next morning. That's the day we were to climb way up into the wildflower meadow and alpine tundra surrounding the first of two stunningly beautiful mountain lakes on Canada's west coast — the Rainbow Lake on the Madely Trail — a truly arduous six-hour uphill hike into Paradise.

52 *Rainbow Madely Trail*

We jumped out of bed at 8 AM Monday, somewhat hung over from the previous night's excitement. After several litres of OJ and a breakfast of porridge and toast with peanut butter and jam, we headed down to the Rainbow Lake trailhead,

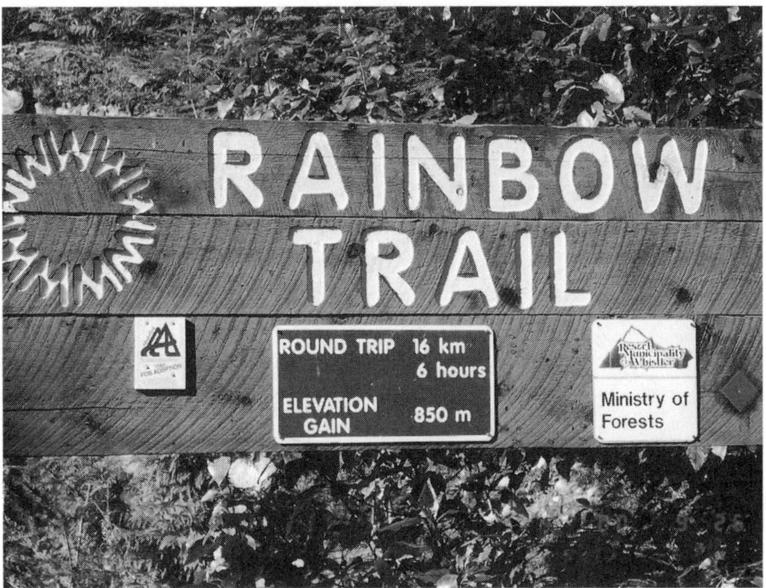

just past the Whistler Cemetery on Alta Lake Road, south of Whistler Creek and west off Highway 99. The elevation at trailhead is 660 metres. That day we would be climbing a fairly rugged and vertical trail to 1,500 metres; that's just under 5,000 feet. The Rainbow Madely winds up the mountains among the giant Douglas firs and hemlocks of the coastal forest, where three hours later, we came upon the most tranquil, clear alpine lake I've ever had the exhausted pleasure to visit. Now's a good time to demonstrate to you the graphic difference between Kayak Mike, a supremely healthy 25-year-old glacier guide, and Hiker Mike, living inside a not-so-bad 55-year-old corpus which, because of various body-contact sports, has seen better days. Arriving at Rainbow Lake after an exceedingly strenuous three-hour uphill boot, I found a grassy knoll beside the lake and fell over, spread-eagled, face down for the lunch hour. Kayak Boy, meanwhile, divested himself of his big backpack (he was carrying all the water and food for both of us, while I was carrying my extra socks and a Mars bar). He then grabbed his camera box and a litre of H_20 and literally ran up the mountain overlooking the lake by some 150 metres to take some wildflower pictures in the alpine tundra above. He woke me up an hour later with a bunch of dried fruit, trail mix and chocolate.

Rainbow Lake is the source of Whistler's drinking water, so though it's almost 10K away from the village, bathing or camping lakeside is forbidden. I've never seen water so clear; the signs and warnings to hikers and backpackers must be working.

We took a bunch of pix for the record. Then, around 2 PM, we started heading back down the trail to our car, way far away — 9K — at Alta Lake Road. Sounds like a cakewalk, eh? Head back down to the car, an easy tumble down the trail, right? Have you ever tried walking downhill for any length of time? Do you know what happens to your toes all jammed up in the front of your boots? How about crippling your quadriceps, wounding your knees, not to mention cramping up your calves. The pain and misery does not go away for three solid hours. I swear to God I'll never bitch and moan about going uphill again. You see, mountain hiking's a big fat trade-off. On your way up you've got to watch your feet otherwise you'll fall on your face. There's not much to see anyway with your back to the view. But once your legs and lungs are used to the pace, into the golden groove you go. The reward is the arrival at the top, the gift of the astonishing view, and the accomplishment of the successful climb. You'll also get to look where you're going all the way back down to your car. But wait about an hour into the descent, when those little toes start squishing up against that unforgiving boot front and the tendons and ligaments around your kneecaps start screaming for mercy. Just wait. Anybody got a hot tub?

There are two ways to take the hike to Rainbow Lake, one of which is a two-car hike-through from Alta Lake Road past Rainbow Lake to Madely Lake Recreation Reserve parking lot. Or do what we did. Hike up to the lake and back down to the cemetery. Both hikes are six hours, so please take plenty of water. Even though you're hiking all the way up beside Whistler's watershed, the water is not treated. Giardia, an *E. coli*-like bug, has been found in the area.

For those of you backpackers and day hikers who resent paying $300 a night to stay in Whistler, there's a great hostel, four to a room, on Alta Lake Road just before the cemetery. So save your money and make lots of like-minded friends from around the world.

When we got back to the chalet, a couple of lobsters were thrown onto the 'Q, ready to be pillaged and eaten by two exceedingly ravenous Hiker Mikes — Allison and Kirby. Ho hum, another day on the mountain trails. Just like Maggie Muggins says, "Tra laa laa laa laa laa lorrow, I wonder what will happen tomorrow?"

53 *B.C. Trail Rules*

B.C. mountain hiking is quite different from what we're used to in the East. The hiking is far more sophisticated, favouring the backpacker, with one hell of a lot more rules to follow. I resented all the damn regulations at first, but eventually came to realize that rules are for our safety and protect the pristine ecosystems that we hikers pass through. I laughed at the large number of outhouses on the trail. They're everywhere! I'm used to stepping well off the trail and doing my business, but then I realized that there must be hundreds of thousands of hikers passing through these trails, and I was outraged when I began to see toilet paper, soiled Kleenex and Wet Ones right next to the pathway. What stupid, insensitive bastards, I thought. Why in hell are these morons not using the outhouses? The sign suggests that in an emergency you dig a hole in a dry area at least 100 metres away from any water course, pop your poop in the hole and cover afterward.

And there are more rules you'll come to know and love while hiking B.C. No dogs. Can you believe that? Dogs were made for hiking, especially in these bear-infested environs. Why, one morning as we prepared to leave the chalet back at Whistler, this large, fat bear was sitting in the bushes beside our kitchen door, and if it weren't for the neighbour's dog setting up the hue and cry, we would have tripped over the big bugger on our way to the car. Hope the pictures turn out so you'll know I'm not lying. Biggest, widest black-bear snout I ever did see. So I don't agree with the "no dog" rule on the trail.

Because the distances are so great and trails pass through remote and hard-to-get-to wilderness areas, hikers like us must

think ahead. Always carry the essentials and be prepared to stay outdoors overnight. It is also a good idea to write down a trip plan and leave it with a friend. Make sure it's a friend because if you don't come back on time he might not tell anybody! Stick to your turnaround time, because it's a true bitch hiking B.C. trails in the dark. Always hike with a buddy and keep together by travelling at the slower hiker's speed. If you do get lost, stay where you are and don't move off the trail or you'll be really lost. Build a fire, sing some Broadway showtunes, and make a shelter to protect yourself from the hungry bears and cougars (preferably a steel cage suspended from a tall tree). Make yourself very visible during daylight hours, or you can do what I do and just sit down, have a good cry, put your head between your legs and kiss your ass goodbye. I know I've used that saying before, but it's just so damned apropos.

54 *Stuff to Bring*

Try to carry a map of the area and a compass, along with a flashlight and extra batteries. I always take a hat and some UV bug spray when I can remember. You know those big orange plastic bags for gathering leaves? They make a great raincoat if you punch a few holes in them, or a lean-to tarp if you split the bag along the seams. A little extra food and water, a pocket knife, some matches and a candle, and most of all, a first-aid kit — all worth their extra weight if you ever find yourself badly lost out there on the Big Ball. Forewarned is forearmed, my hearties! And never, never, never step off the trail, because you'll kill all the baby plants and their moms will be really pissed at you and then you'll never get out alive.

55 *Garibaldi Lake and the Black Tusk*

Day 4 dawned with a surprise visit from our generous host, Jim Tutton. Jim had suggested that we climb the big trail to Garibaldi Glacier Lake, with an eye towards an assault on the Black Tusk after lunch. So he jammed a big pack full of lunch and water and drove us 23 kilometres south of Whistler Creek to the trailhead on Highway 99, where under a clear sky we began a gradual three-hour climb up a wide and welcoming trail, switching back and forth through the giant Douglas firs, until we came at last to the glistening shores of the aquamarine and sky-blue waters of Garibaldi Lake, surrounded by treed and tundra mountains on all sides and featuring the volcano's cinder core of the Black Tusk overhead. But the showpiece, front and centre, directly across the lake from our lunch on Battleship Point, through the islands in the middle distance, was snow-capped Deception Peak and the great Sphinx Glacier, whose icy pathway flowed down towards us into the terminal face, a massive jumble of boulders at the water's edge. We took lots of pictures over a lunch of dried fruit, nuts and juicy oranges, while the whiskey jacks — those friendly little birds — landed on our fingers and ate from our palms. Oh so gently, but bold as brass, the little buggers would puff out their cheeks filled with all the trail mix they could carry.

We realized as we sat and looked up at the Black Tusk, some 5 to10K to the north of us, that we would have to wait for another time to make the climb. Too much for one day. The Tusk itself is a volcanic cone of black granite shaped like a rhino's tusk or a giant black finger that beckoned us to come up and say "Hello." The mountain on which the Tusk sits has been worn away by nature, leaving only the "tusk."

If you're a backpacker, the best way to make the round trip to Garibaldi Lake, then on to the Black Tusk, is to set up camp on the first day at the Taylor Campgrounds — a three-to-four-hour climb with pack from the trailhead parking lot back on Highway 99. Climb the Tusk on Day 2, then on Day 3 break camp and walk down to Garibaldi Lake for lunch, then back to your car at a leisurely pace.

The Garibaldi Lake Hike is within reach of all hikers, even the most inexperienced, as long as you stay on the trail. Kayak Mike's parents walked up to the lake on their honeymoon. Take your time and follow the well-marked and wide trail and enjoy the mountain majesty that the B.C. parks afford you.

We cleared the Black Tusk Trail around 4 PM, after our three-hour downhill meander back to the car, all the while discussing the Fed's decision to change Mt. Logan to Mt. Trudeau. Outdoor people in B.C., it seems, have a thorough knowledge of the history and accomplishments of the geologist-adventurer Logan, and are not too enthusiastic about his mountain being taken away from him by government decree. In order to smooth Hiker Jim Tutton's ruffled political ledges, I suggested that we have filet mignon, corn on the cob and several bottles of fine merlot, all to be consumed at my expense back at the Whistler Chalet. We all responded, "Yes to Everything," and proceeded swiftly through the rush-hour traffic back to Whistler Creek for an evening of gourmet debauchery under the twin summits of Whistler and Blackcombe Mountains.

56 *Tofino — Long Beach Hiking*

When I started to plan my B.C. Blitz day-hiking expedition to Vancouver, Whistler and Tofino, it was only natural that I call Clarence Rosevear, the friendly boot rep at New Balance, to see if he had the proper boot for the B.C. mountains and rainforest. Clarence gave me a waterproof, red, high-top

boot made of rich Corinthian leather, called the 5700 Storm Cloud 7, a most soft and supple leather built on top of a true traction sole, that not only adhered to the most difficult B.C. trails, but looked quite smart and stylish when out searching for salmon steaks at some of Whistler's more sophisto restaurants. Wolf whistles and catcalls were aimed directly at my feet — most embarrassing. But the true test for these Storm Cloud 7s came into play out at Long Beach, south of Tofino, on Vancouver Island, on an exceedingly wet afternoon. In order to get to the beach from the parking lot, Kayak Mike Allison and I had to negotiate a giant log jam — mammoth, slick, barkless logs all cross-hatched in a mishmash, sometimes piled high 10 to 15 feet above the rocks and sand.

There was nothing to do but navigate very carefully along the length of these logs, sometimes jumping in the pummeling rain from one to the other. Lack of traction for a second could have sent me careening down through the logs to the rocks below, broken bones the only reward for my foolhardy efforts. But it just didn't happen, hikers. I felt like a professional log roller, tap dancing my way, albeit very carefully at first, then more confidently as I began to trust the traction these Storm Cloud 7s afforded me. We hiked six to eight hours a day for a week on our B.C. Blitz, and my feet never got sore, my Achilles heels didn't flare up, as they are apt to do on long treks, and my little toes didn't get all jammed up on the lengthy downhill sections of the rough-and-tumble trails. And I didn't go over on my ankles, not once.

BAHAMAS R AND R: The Payoff

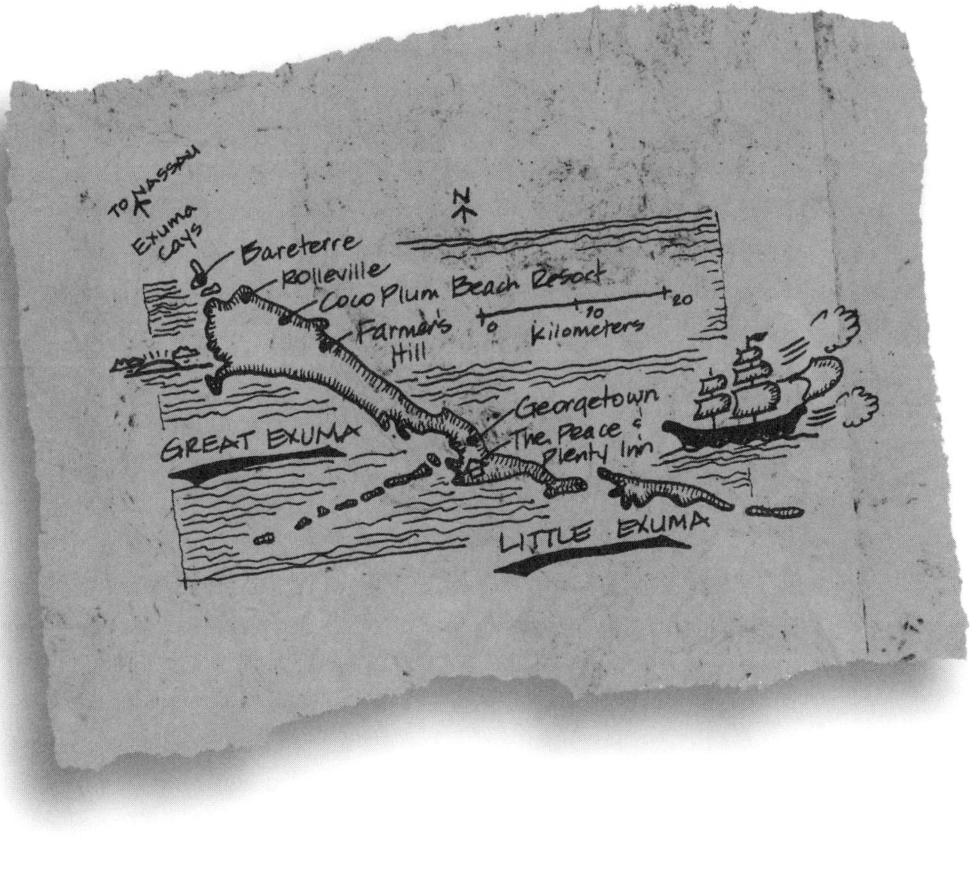

57 *A Salty Story*

June 1975. It was my first time ever to the tropics. I was riding the crest of a burgeoning film-acting career and had been hired by ABC Television to play the guest villain in a short-lived failure called *Salty the Sea Lion*, the follow-up sequel to the hit series *Flipper*. The show was being shot in Nassau, that free-wheeling pirate town on the island of New Providence, capital of the Bahamas, 90 miles across the Gulf Stream from Miami, Florida.

When the Air Canada door flew open, upon disembarking I was smashed in the face with hot, heavy ocean air, that literally took my breath away. This new biospheric excitement carried me out of the plane and into the waiting crew bus, along the green and blue of the palm-fringed oceanside boulevards, all the way to the Montague Beach Hotel and up into my suite of rooms. In the spacious foyer, perched happily on a rounded Duncan Fife table, were a welcoming vase of flowers, a joint of the finest Colombian reefer, a fruit basket, and a bottle of rum, with a note saying, "Welcome to our Salty Family."

After briefly sampling all of the above and changing into my skimpy summer attire, I left the beautifully appointed apartment and descended to the lobby in search of the restaurant. It was right then that I saw a series of steps ascending into the blue Bahamian sky. A good place, thought I, for a restaurant. But as I reached the top step, I came upon a gigantic, crystal-clear swimming pool, completely empty except for a very lonely little sea lion named Salty, who was dying for someone to play with. I've always loved both the water and sea lions — they're just like doggies, only they swim better. So I ripped off all my clothes and dove in to cavort nudely with my new barking friend.

Well, folks, I must have played every underwater game I knew over the next hour or so, including pushing off from the side of the pool and sailing like Superman underwater across the pool while good old Salty fit himself into the small of my back and propelled us both hither and yon. You can imagine just how hungry I was becoming after all this sport. It only took me five minutes to dry my naked body in the tropical sun before I got dressed, said goodbye to my new sea-lion pal (promising to see him on the set real soon), and headed down to the restaurant in search of food, loads of food, as a horrible case of the munchies had kicked in.

My nose followed the good smells to a large, cool and dark bistro where, as luck would have it, the entire crew was having lunch. They rose to their feet cheering as I entered. It wasn't until my eyes became accustomed to the dark of the restaurant that I realized that the walls of the restaurant were the walls of the upstairs swimming pool, with great underwater windows, so the diners could eat and enjoy the swimmers. I had been swimming bare balls naked with a sea lion for the past lunch hour and all the cast and crew were now as familiar with my body's imperfections as my ex-girlfriend Roxy! The joke was on me, but they quickly made me feel part of their Salty Family, once the royal flush of scarlet left my cheeks — all four of them.

We'd been dreaming about this journey for years, and now we were booked. Saturday, November 28, to Sunday, December 5, 2000, we were finally going to hike the full 120 miles of white-and-pink sandbars called the Exuma chain, sitting in the aquamarine Bahamian Sea, just 70 miles southeast of Nassau.

We had flown over this glistening chain o' diamonds countless times in the '70s and '80s as apprentice scuba divers, heading south to Stella Maris on Long Island in the Bahamas, to test ourselves on the world's only shark dive. This is where groups of fearless idiots like myself would spear reef fish and offer them to the more aggressive bull sharks, who'd circle you closer and closer until they worked up the courage to come right up to you and rip the large wriggling grouper, in the midst of his death dance, right off the spear.

My dive buddy, Captain Mike Colbert, a hard-drinking Air Canada 747 pilot, had me stand over him in 30 feet of water while he lay on his belly on the bottom of the ocean and filmed the bull-shark feeding frenzy. My job was to fend off the big, nosy bastards with a small prod stick when they came too close to Captain Mike's camera. That I've even survived this ordeal and lived to tell you about it is a miracle in itself. But more on the Stella Maris shark dive and Dorothy the Golden Shiksa, who would give me everything if I would only marry her, at a more appropriate time. Those countless 50-minute fly-overs from Nassau to Long Island (Stella Maris) afforded me a special viewing opportunity, at 1,500 feet from the Cessna cockpit, down the long scimitar-like archipelago called Exuma.

I could never complete that magical passage, flying southeast of Nassau in the late morning, with the sun bouncing off the pastel blues and greens of the hundreds of Exuma islands, quays and lagoons, without dreaming about hiking those sand bars from end to end one day, when I had the time to explore at a more leisurely pace.

So it was with already rising excitement that my buddy Captain Karl Pruner, successful film actor and Urban Sherpa, and yours truly, booked passage to New Providence. The adventure will take us to downtown Nassau, where we'd hopefully locate a mail boat cum freighter to take us the four hours over to the top of the Exuma chain. Then we'd hike our way south through the islands' roads and pathways, taking a water taxi or hiring a boat when the ocean got in the way, until we came to Great Exuma at the bottom, and Georgetown, the ancient buccaneer capital of these Bahamian paradise out islands.

Who knew if we'd make it all the way to Georgetown? There must be many uninhabited or privately owned islands in the chain. Were the islands close enough together so that we can swim from one to the other? Were the currents between the islands too strong and dangerous as the ocean waters ripped into the leeward lagoons? How was the wildlife in the reefs just offshore? Bull sharks are prevalent in the shallow, rich coral gardens where there's plenty of food, and bull sharks are very territorial. They don't like big animals (like swimmers!) invading the reef, their kitchen and dining room.

Lots of questions to answer — the joy of the mystery journey. I try to do only basic research when I prepare for a voyage. Some travellers take the journey by way of library, video and the Internet so that they know what to expect upon arrival. I like to get off the plane at a strange airport and find my way from there, normally by locating a like-minded taxi man who, for a fee, will escort you to a great restaurant, show you the best beach for swimming, then head you over to his Aunt Madelinas Guest House for a good night's sleep. It's the journey into the unknown that's exciting for me, handing over the reins to the Goddess Fortuna, who most times raises you up but sometimes smashes you down (that's the Bitch Goddess Fortuna). One of the good slogans to live by, according to all my pals at AA, is to, "Let go and let Goddess." So we put the journey in Fortuna's hands to see where we would end up. Yes to Everything!

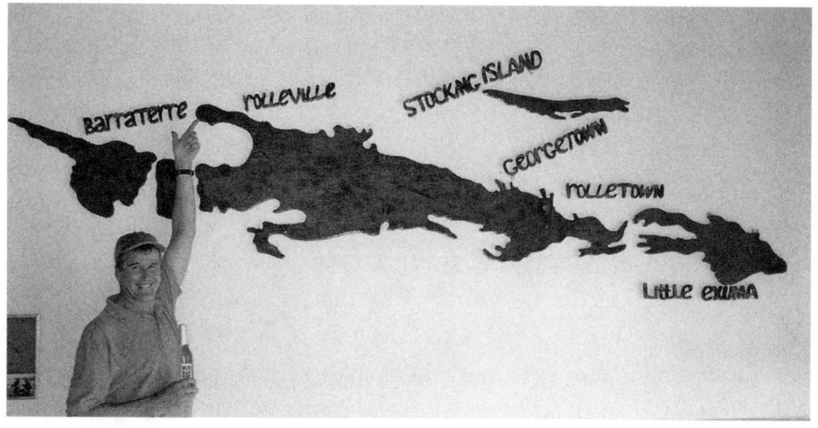

Pen Pal: Liz, the Chain Of Diamonds, and Great Exuma

"I would love to read more about your experiences in Exuma. My husband and I were there 15 years ago when the island was 'way off the beaten track.' We stayed for 2 weeks and covered every inch of Little and Great Exuma on motorcycles. I would love to return; but I am always afraid I might be just a wee bit disappointed (you can never go back syndrome)." — *Liz Ritchie*

"Not only can you go back, you must go back." — *HM*

58 *Pulling My Luck in Funky Nassau*

I was sitting with my feet up in the cool shade of an open window, gazing incredulously out onto the sparkling Bahamian water, after a hearty lunch of snapper fish and vegetables and a heaping big bowl of conch salad. The Captain had just gone down to Cable Beach on the west end of Nassau to procure some rolling papers to go with the little taste of herb that Jerry the Rasta Man pressed upon us earlier that morning, down at the harbour under the Rainbow Bridge leading to Paradise Island.

We had been snooping around the harbour master's office trying to book passage on the *Etienne and Cyphus* mail boat bound for the Exuma out islands, where we planned to hike for the next week. But as luck would have it (and if you're a regular here in the Bahamas, you quickly realize that luck has everything to do with it), the package did not set sail till Tuesday at 2 PM. Since we didn't want to waste two whole days of our allotted seven hanging around dirty old Nassau, we decided to jump on board a Bahamas Air prop jet that day at 4 PM and scoot over to Great Exuma to begin our hike adventure immediately. So we stopped in at the Government Land and Survey Department and had the nice people print up a map of the entire 120-mile chain of all the Exuma Keys, in order to find out which islands were private, uninhabited and roadworthy. Our taxi man was waiting for us outside the Ministry, and while backing up to turn his van around, as luck would have it, came a large tree branch through his rear window, shattering the glass all over our LoweAlpine Vision 40 backpacks. I did mention this luck thing earlier, didn't I?

We had our lunch at Fish Fries Bahamian Restaurant, just off West Bay Street, where taxi man dropped us while he had the van repaired. We awaited his return, but he never showed up, so we called the airport limo and got to the airport and over to the next leg of our adventure — Great Exuma.

Just as I expected, the top 60 miles of the enchanted Exumas were either private cays, national parks (no trespassing) or drug lords' Brunei-type, fully armed fortress islands. So the best we could do was to fly to Georgetown, on Great Exuma, the big island at the bottom of the chain, and take a taxi north to where the road begins at Barreterre. And that is exactly what we did. But first we were going to spend a night or two at the splendid old sailor's hotel in Georgetown called Peace and Plenty. After clearing Customs upon arrival, we told our Exuma taxi man, Kermit Rolle, what we had planned. Kermit asked us instead to be his guests at his humble home up Rolleville way, just to the southeast of where we wanted to start our hike. Yes, of course Kermit, we'd be honoured, we thought, to share your one-room cottage with you, your wife and three kids. Kermit was, we assumed, a man of modest means. Although he looked quite handsome — Sidney Poitier with a moustache and dancing eyes — his dress was most assuredly workaday.

So imagine our astonishment when we climbed the highest hill on the island and there, atop the crest, stood a large and gracious Liz-Taylor-type villa with water on all sides. We were led to a Grand Salon the size of an ambassador's living room and then into our own suite, among a carpeted series of guest quarters, with two bedrooms and private washrooms. All rooms opened at either end by means of great sliding-glass doors, allowing the Bahama winter winds to pass through at their whim. Now as I lay writing this description, surrounded by darkness, I

had yet to see the castle grounds in the light. I could only guess by the sound of the distant pounding of the surf and the harsh rattle of the numerous royal palm fronds that the grounds of Kermit's Point were immense.

Kermit's Villa, Tuesday morning. As I emerged from my sleeping quarters onto a stark white temple balcony overlooking the azure sea filled with countless baby Exuma cays, I was greeted by a short but tiny, perfect, nut-brown version of an old Greek-style god. "My name is Hanno," he said, his long, fine, white mane and beard blasted by the wind, his green eyes blazing. "Isn't it wonderful to be alive when the sun is shining? It's been raining a great deal lately, what with the hurricanes, so I stay next door to you! Normally I live in the caves down there next to the beach," he said, pointing to a rocky but well-pined hummock rising out of the sea. "I don't wear clothes here as there is no one, so you and your friend must feel free to do the same."

Hanno couldn't have been more than 5 feet tall and, at best, 100 pounds. He wore nothing but a faded red bikini. His body was lean and tanned golden brown, except for a blanket of thick white hair from his breast to his bollocks. His look was lithe and sinewy, with an elegance and grace to his movements. He proceeded to show us the grounds, where the roads led, where the surf was best, and where to pick the papaya, banana and mango. Hanno also shared with us the location of his secret lagoon — a nylon pool where the water was so clear as to appear invisible — until you touched it.

Hanno's 80-year-old eyes would lock onto yours when he spoke of "the evil of civilized man," who cannot live side by side with Nature on our Big Ball, and even here, away from city and town, he held up proof to us. On his feet he showed us the oil tar from walking on the beach, the shiny black gook having been flushed out of the bilge or thrown overboard from passing ships. Hanno was 19 years old in 1939 and had fought in both Africa and Russia for Hitler's Third Reich. He survived, and with his family moved to Minnesota, where he was given tenure as a professor of history at St. Olaf's College for his working life. Now, at 80 years of age, Hanno walked great distances along the ocean, regularly hugged his friends the trees, and sang loudly from atop the hills, danced with both joy and sorrow while the sun smiled and watched. He would make a fine neighbour.

After a light breakfast of coffee and Snickers bars, Captain Karl and I put on our Timberland water hikers, our sunglasses and a little nose coat, and headed down the hill, south to the shallows of the tidal lagoon, a mile-long crescent bay of white-pink coral sands and baby-blue liquids. There we watched another new friend, Lindsay, bone-fishing. This is an extremely difficult and exasperating sport, demanding lightning-quick reaction time in order to catch the "ghost fish," whose colors are those of the sandy bottom against which they hide. Lindsay said if we hurried we could hike the narrow beach out around the headland, but the tide would be coming soon, so we mustn't delay. I had a feeling that Lindsay was either sending us to our deaths or he was just trying to get rid of us. It didn't matter. Yes to Everything! So off we went down the chalky sliver of silver beach whose headland point lay ahead of us a good half mile.

Splooshing along towards the point with gentle waves washing over our feet, we noticed the mangoes and the papaya trees thriving splendidly on the south-facing island slope, along with the broad-leafed sea grape, often used as a sculpted windbreak on a beach house's front yard. We also saw the Queen of the Bahamas trees — the sea pine. Strong, stately and graceful, the feathery branches of the sea pines whisper the poetry of the wind. Her wood, used for building houses, petrifies to stone after a hundred years, allowing it to stand up to hurricanes, high winds and salt erosion.

As we approached the headland point from the south, we noticed the beach growing narrower and the wind blowing more strongly as the damned water got deeper and deeper. The razor-sharp ironstone coral of the shore became impassable. Would we be able to traverse the point without leaving our feet or having to swim to safety around the point? We began carrying our cameras and bags above our heads, but swimming would just not do, so I handed the Captain my stuff and I forged on ahead to check out the depths and possibilities for safe passage.

As I closed on the point, an insouciant ocean wave slapped my face and sent me reeling backwards off my feet, filling my morning eyes with stinging salty fluids. The high tide had beaten us to the point. There was nothing for it but to retrace our steps back down the beach from whence we had come and admit defeat (albeit a small one) to the God of the Deeps. The next day we would wait for low tide and do this hike properly.

Bahamian winters are cool and windy, comparable perhaps to early May in Canada. Noon hours reach 20–22°C, but the nights can be downright chilly. However, this weather is heavenly tropical for Canadian Norsemen. We think nothing of wearing shorts and sneakers with our favourite old t-shirt, but all the local Exumans laugh behind their hands when they see the white-skinned Canucks cavorting in the icy December surf. They wouldn't dream of sticking in their little toes until June.

The Bahamian winter expresses herself emotionally by sudden and violent torrents of blustery night air. You may look up and see the stars sparkling clearly above you and at the same time wonder where in hell's name is the rain hitting your face coming from. Simple. It's been blown at you by Aeolus, the Great Northern God of Wind, an ever-present winter visitor to the Bahamian out islands.

I do not wish to make you think that Aeolus is not welcome, for the wind changes the face of the otherwise hazy pastels of the summers, making the colours extremely sharp by contrast. The skyline of the distant islands is a sea-pine green, underlined by a sharp white gash of pure coral sand, which in turn kisses the soft nylon pool shallows before giving over to the aquamarine, then the inky indigo of the deeps, stampeding headlong into the horizon. The pinks and purples of the balloon-like clouds scooting by just above belong in a Casper the Friendly Ghost cartoon.

One of the earlier conversations I had had with the naked Hanno while he danced in the morning sun, his snow-white bollocks bouncing rhythmically in time to the music of the spheres, was about the Silence of the Exumas. "Don't you find the solitude and silence wonderful?" he asked. "I'm sure I would," I responded, "if we could only get the wind to shut the fuck up for a minute!"

Aeolus rules on Exuma, folks. The God of the Wind keeps all living things flexible with continuous motion. Waves of long grass rolled past my feet as I stood on the white Athenian balcony, looking out to sea. The wind was everywhere, howling happily through an open doorway behind me, making the shrubbery dance and chatter madly in the garden, obliging the palm frond and the sea-pine branches to bow courteously to one another. The plants and animals are made stronger, more pliant, supple and even smarter for having to deal with the strength of the wind. I watched as a wily young hummingbird actually landed on a long, quickly moving wildflower stalk, in order to suck on the sweetness, while riding the plant violently back and forth in Mother Nature's rodeo. The winter wind, though coolly benign, is the constant theme in the Exuman movie track. I have a feeling you must wait for the still and sultry summer to enjoy the silence here.

I spent some time once in the Aegean Sea, on the island of Mykonos, and the strongest memory I took away was the light-show of shade and colour that the sun and the clouds imposed on the waters and neighbouring islands. The constant change was both startling to the eye and unsettling to the spirit. The colour of the vista would transform in an instant, causing one to question the veracity of what one saw only moments ago. In the Bahamas, the water will do the same to you. The Inuit have hundreds of names for snow, and the same could well apply to the waters of the Exumas. Coral heads, blue holes, sand bars and ocean trenches all have their own exciting colour swatch of blue that'll steal your breath away. Your eyes will drown with pleasure as you succumb to the countless hues of blues.

It is now the golden twilight of evening, and the men have gathered in the Grand Salon of Kermit's villa for cocktails and hors d'oeuvres, rum-and-Cokes, large pieces of fresh coconut, and little baby bananas freshly picked from the backyard. Kermit Rolle, our host and benefactor taxi guy, has returned to cook us a dinner surprise. Kermit exudes grace, humility and wit. He is a descendant of slaves whose forebearers were rewarded in 1834 by the Governor Sir John Rolle with not only their freedom but also with a collective grant of 6,500 acres in the Exumas, well before the Civil War. The slaves in turn took Sir John's surname as their own, in honour of this generous gent. Pointing to the centre of the living room, Kermit told me that as a boy he would come to this very spot, and right there where the coffee table is now stood an immense boulder, onto which he would climb and sit, dreaming that one day, as a man, he would build his house on top of this hill among the fruit trees, high above the sea. The boy went in the direction of his dreams, as Thoreau once said, and Kermit is living the life he imagined.

We finished off our first day in Exuma with Kermit's dinner surprise: giant lobster tails, succulent and sweet, baked peas and rice, and an apple-and-lettuce salad. Hanno would not join us at dinner because we were eating flesh carcass, and Hanno ate only fruit and veggies grown in full view of sun and sky. Hiker Mike took his weary old bones to bed at 8:20 PM and, snuggling in with Bill Bryson's *Notes from a Small Island* balanced warmly on his chest, proceeded to weigh anchor and sail off towards Wednesday morning with the Bahamian winter wind blowing full into the starched white sails of his dream boat.

Wednesday I rolled over and out of a deep sleep at 6:20 AM, and through the open window I watched the naked imp Hanno attempt to throw a rather large coconut husk out across the green and into the bushes. The hairy little monkey skull smashed instead onto the archway of the porch above the little elf's head, landing quietly at his feet. Hanno laughed delightedly, scooped up the disobedient coco husk, broke into a German marching song and carried his wounded friend back into his room. Thus began Day 2 on my windy island hilltop in Exuma.

59 *I Wasn't Meant to Carry a Backpack*

Let's go back to the beginning of this adventure for a moment. And speaking of backs, somewhere between the bed at the Montague Beach Hotel in Nassau and the plane ride to Great Exuma, I am less than happy to report, my lower back went on strike. While departing on the Bahamas Air 4:20 flight to Georgetown, Captain Karl made mention that I was listing distinctly to port.

"Nonsense!" I responded, "It's only because I'm carrying my backpack!"

"Nonsense!" retorted the Captain. "You're not wearing a backpack!"

Bad sign! First my lower-left vertebrae simply slide out of whack from physical abuse, then the muscles seize up around the injured area. I generally can't move for a day or two until I can work the tension out of my back and the spasms stop. This little mobility problem kind of redefined the 20-mile-a-day hiking trip we were here to do on Great Exuma. But here's how it played itself out the first few days.

I went down for the count, and I mean flat out. Good ol' pal Captain Karl took care of all the logistics — backpacks, groceries, meal preparation, and cocktail mixing (my favorite cocktail is the herb spritzer — sweetgrass and Perrier). We had the good fortune to be sharing a great suite of rooms with sliding glass walls on both ends, so the Captain moved my big bed over to the wall, took down the curtains and made a fort high above the sea, into which I crawled with books, cigars, my radio and my "Notables" 8-by-10 writing tablet. I didn't leave the fort, other than to crawl on my hands and knees to the bathroom or to go out onto the hot concrete patio to lie naked in the Caribbean sun doing stretching and relaxation exercises. After a couple of days of treating myself like precious cargo, I moved into a comfy, bobbing, contoured chair for reading, writing and good conversation with Kermit, the ever-gracious Captain and that 80-year-old singing madman Hanno. Hanno took a particular shine to the Hiker because I love to walk and eat bananas, just like him. The back took three to four days of my seven-day vacation to heal itself, but I don't get frustrated by what others might consider a misadventure. I certainly don't feel I wasted any time on my back. I was either talking or relaxing with good friends, or just going into the waking dream on my own, losing myself out there. Although I must admit that my impatient spirit was exhorting my body to "Hurry the hell up and heal" so we could get moving down the road again.

Wednesday afternoon Fortuna smiled on me. We came back from a boisterous, wave-tossing swim in the Big Blue and my back was back. The bones were unlocked down at the bottom of my lower left, and the muscles had ceased their protective spasms. But though my body was loosened up and relaxed, I still felt weak. A good night's sleep was in order to put me on the comeback trail the next morning for the 6-mile round-trip foray into the depths of the Rolleville village centre for lunch. Thank you, Fortuna.

After a short rest back at the villa, complete with coffee and a good read of Thomson Highway's *Kiss of the Fur Queen*, an absolute mesmerizer, I waited for sunset to walk gingerly back down to the sea along the steep, coral-paved driveway. Following the road to the end, I stepped onto the endless sandbar stretching out to where the sun's orange explosion met the sea. The sandbar was a silver-and-pink opalescent ocean highway, made luminous under the red pastels of the gathering night clouds. The north wind blew cool on my face, while the receding tidewater warmed my feet. The sun's disappearance left me only 15 more minutes of light and the promise of a beautiful tomorrow.

60 *The Ocean Swim*

Thursday we started out the day with a little swim. We'd been toying with the idea of hiking the sandbars at low tide, along the coast and around the jungle peninsula that juts straight out into the ocean waves like a giant thumb before curling back to the sheltered beach on the lee side. The journey seemed quite simple, apart from one unknown fact. How tough and how deep would the water be at the peninsula's point, where the peaceful Bahamian lagoon clashes with the full frenzy of the North Atlantic? Would the waves be powerful enough to blow us ashore, carving us into hamburger on the razor-sharp coral rocks? Or would we be pulled out to sea by the tide and the backwash of the waves?

And so, armed with only our scuba masks and underpants, we set forth, following the sandy shore of the silent lagoon. We were a good quarter mile to the open water when we noticed that it was getting deeper with every step, so very little time passed before we were breaststroking our way into an ever-freshening headwind. Although the lagoon's surface was becoming quite choppy, we were able to dive down and swim along the bottom while holding our breath, using our masks' clear vision to maintain direction and observe the wildlife: coral heads, beds of seaweed and small schools of yellowtail, the odd

conch shell being pulled along the sandy bottom by a large black claw extending from its pink pearly opening. But as we began to round the peninsula point, we were met by a violent wind worthy of Cape Horn, which had every intention of throwing us onto the rocks, thus ending both our swim and our lives. We quickly compensated by swimming away from shore and into the teeth of the screaming gale and the rolling waves. It was right then that both Captain Karl and I realized that we were being sucked out to sea by the backwash from the waves hitting the rocks, and in minutes, with a little bad luck, we could be miles from shore.

We could see the beach a few hundred yards ahead, where we intended to come ashore, but we couldn't get to it directly so we decided to swim parallel to the shore with the razor rocks on our right and the mighty ocean's pull to our left, hoping that once we were clear of the point, the maelstromic meeting of the two bodies of water would dissipate and the ocean would calm itself once again. And thank Fortuna, we guessed correctly, because not 50 yards past the stormy point, Captain and I were engulfed by a large magnanimous wave that gently spewed us up onto the welcoming pink beach. As we stood, sand-coated from head to butt, looking back at where we'd been, we were grateful once again to be out of harm's way.

To celebrate the successful circumnavigation of the rough peninsula, we walked back up to the villa for PB & J sandwiches. After a short rest we decided that, in order to make the journey around the headland our very own, we would go back down to the dock and swim back the way we had come, retracing our strokes into the windy sea. Back around the point to the sandbar, this time buck naked, sans mask, sans trunks or water shoes, clad only in our watches and large, salty smiles. Our Good Mother the Sea was much kinder to us the second time around.

After the round-trip swim, my lower back seemed relaxed enough for our first lengthy trek into Rolleville, 5 kilometres away, past fields of corn and fruit trees. The good and level road led us inland, rising gently to the east, and delivered us to the serenity of a small, quiet village, full of brightly painted pastel cottages and the sounds of the school kids in uniform

playing ball in the friendly streets and jungle backyards. We were looking for chocolate, chips and Cokes, so the kids were very helpful, showing us personally where these treasures were to be found. Imagine our surprise when the bar cum restaurant cum candy store turned out to be Kermit's Hilltop Café; the man who owns our villa also owns several other business concerns in Rolleville. Kermit's brother Clayton took excellent care to pack up our confections in a nice big box, including two large coconuts for our roommate Hanno. Then he asked his nephew, Santonio, to drive us the 5K back to the villa. These generosities are common to Exumans. They're always one step ahead in helping a newcomer, which made our island stay most pleasant.

During the drive back to the villa, Santonio told us that every child born in Rolleville was entitled to a generous piece of land as his or her birthright, handed down by their benefactor, Lord John Rolle, who had tried to make it up to the slaves hiding in Great Exuma for the hideous wrong doings committed against them. This "grant to the people" took place in 1832, almost 30 years before the American Civil War in which Lincoln fought for the emancipation of all people in the Americas. Lord Rolle was blessedly ahead of his time.

Thursday night, Kermit came home with three fat Cornish game hens, dead of course, which he proceeded to stuff with bread, celery, onions and spices, and we all sat down to a grand dinner. Hanno joined us at table only after the carcasses were dispatched and sang to us his "Song of the Stars." He was quite excited, because just outside, over the villa, Jupiter, Saturn, Mercury and Mars had lined up in a row, and Venus would be joining them at dawn. Unfortunately, I was too exhausted to stay up with them for very long, and I fell asleep in my cozy bed listening to happy laughter and stories on into the quiet night, while Hanno sang praise to the heavens through his flowing white beard.

Friday was a truly magical day. Captain Karl began with a swim in the lagoon at low tide, where he was surrounded by a prodigious herd of several dozen largish manta rays in the sandy shallows just offshore. The rays were all perhaps 2 feet across from wing to wing and sporting a barbed and dangerous tail some 2 to 3 feet in length. The Captain came slowly to a halt and watched quietly as they came to check him out, two abreast, then gently swam around him and continued on their early morning hunt for food.

We decided to walk the 10 miles past Rolleville to the grocery store in Farmer's Hill to replenish our dwindling stock of Cokes and Snickers bars. We had only heard of Farmer's Hill, and didn't really know where it was, but some of the older ladies in Rolleville took a shine to us, aiming us down the right road, so off we strode. It felt great to be back on the road in search of adventure, and it wasn't long before we came to a little curve on a cool jungle hill, and there waiting for us was Winston the woodcarver, who welcomed us warmly to his roadside stall. On display were two dozen beautiful carvings of the different fish from the seas around Exuma — French angels, groupers, bonefish and dolphins, all rendered with an exquisite and realistic touch. Karl bought the dolphin and the fat-lipped grouper. We made mention to Winston and his carving pal Devon that his fish reminded us that we were hungry for lunch, and he pointed us down the beach road to the lagoon, on whose shores stood Darren's Conch Stand, a newly built, carousel-shaped restaurant, surrounded by decks opening out to the sea, filled with comfortable chairs and recliners and round white tables. Darren served us the most succulent whole fish on a bed of plantain, onions and tomatoes. He even offered to drive us the remaining few miles to the grocery store in Farmer's Hill, but since our strength had returned after the fish lunch, we demurred and, thanking him for his offer, hit the road along the azure coast once more.

61 *Serendipity*

Maybe it's because we were hiking on an island and the natives see us coming, but everything seemed to fall into place as if by magic. I'm always surprised and delighted by what appears to be coincidence in the Bahamas. Let me give

you an example. No sooner had we arrived at the grocery store, bought our treats and were checking out at the cash register, when the phone rang behind the counter. The lady cashier answered, listened for a moment, then smiled knowingly at us and said, "Are you Captain Karl and Hiker Mike?"

"Why yes," we sputtered.

"It's for you," said she. Karl took the phone and the woman on the line told him to wait at the store, as Kermit Rolle was on his way to pick us up. We thanked the cashier, picked up our bags of groceries and walked out the door, smack into Kermit, who was pulling up in the taxi van. This kind of delightful coincidence happens all the time in the Bahamas.

We laughed and talked and ate chocolate bars all the way back to the villa, where we stripped down, took our masks and headed down to the beach. Diving off the dock into the ocean's high tide, we were gently pushed around the headland and into the lee of the lagoon. And waiting for us there in the shallows once more were the manta rays, who escorted us to shore just in time for a purple and golden sunset and a perfect ending to another magical day on Great Exuma.

Saturday morning dawned high, bright and blue up top of Kermit's Point, the northern and westernmost tip of Great Exuma. Hanno sang us out of our beds with his happy-sad goodbye song, because he knew we were leaving for Nassau later in the day. We looked at our gear skewed out across our suite of rooms and instantly decided that a sayonara hike and swim were in order before packing and travel prep. Kermit had mentioned a good two-hour hiking combo of road and beach leading south out of Rolleville, only a mile away, so we put on our shoes and shorts, grabbed our camera, and headed down the peninsula towards Rolleville.

Now, Rolleville is famous for more than that excellent land grant every child receives at birth. The very wonderful and talented Esther Rolle and her family were born here. Esther played the maid "Florida" in all those Norman Lear and Bud Yorkin television comedies in the '70s and '80s, including *All in the Family*, *Maude*, and *Movin' on Up*, as well as the ground-breaking, Oscar-winning movie *Driving Miss Daisy*, in which she co-starred with Jessica Tandy, who also lived in Rolleville with her husband Hume Cronyn before her recent death. So the sleepy, pristine village of pastel cottages is used to its share of famous people. The citizens treat famous and non-famous alike with the same friendly outgoing manner.

The owner of the liquor store, a Mr. Rolle, pointed us south out of the village down the road and into the sun. We marched together, the Captain and I, until we reached the second sweeping jungle turn, and there it was, in the bush to our left, buried in the tangle of creeping mangrove vines and sea grape: an old, rotting sign pointing the way to the Coco Plum Beach Resort. We could hear the crash of the waves on the beach beyond the rise some half mile away, but the sandy double rut of a road didn't look too promising as it made a feeble effort to proceed through the swamp ahead. Our fears were soon realized as the road dipped down into a large, dank lake with a limestone bottom, into whose shallows we were forced to wade. We tried to find suitable and dry passage on either side, but the tangle of mangrove jungle was impenetrable, driving us back to the underwater road. So risking a probable reptile attack of poisonous water snakes, we took off our boots and socks and forward we slogged, planting each precious step into the slime most cautiously.

Fortuna was smiling on us, for though the yellow water flirted with our quivering calves, we legged it through without incident. After drying off in the sun on the far shore, we booted up and hiked over the sandy 30-foot rise of Atlantic sand dune and found ourselves on the eastern shore of pink coral beach. Propped above the waves stood the old, abandoned Coco Plum Beach Resort, in all its glorious decay. It broke my heart to see what the weather had done to this old Queen of the Coral Reef. Hurricane Floyd had delivered the final coup de grace to this onetime "party central." The restaurants, dance floor and outhouses were working their way back into nature, but it was easy to see why party people had come from as far away as Nassau and Georgetown to jump up and party down in the resort's heyday. So sad to watch good club go bad.

We walked down the pristine powder of coral sand beach to the aquamarine shallows and turned left. Heading north, we

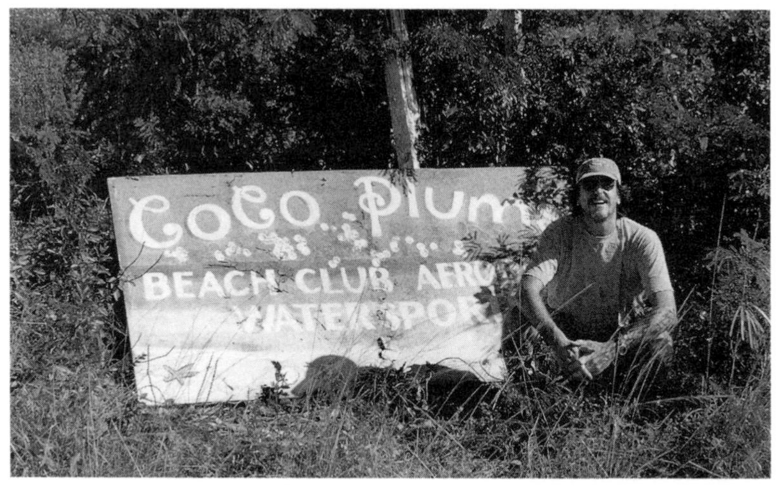

stayed on the hard-packed, close to the waves, and after an hour of pink, green and blue eye candy, we came to the beach houses and cottages of the lucky people of Rolleville. The whole Coco Plum loop took us a little over two hours back to Kermit's villa. We disrobed and jumped into the turbulent ocean waves from the dock and swam around the peninsula headland to the shallows in the lee one last time.

This was the end of our stay in Exuma. We made our sad goodbyes after we packed, took a few pictures of the place and headed down the hill in Kermit's taxi. As I looked back at the villa that gave us five days of joy, I watched Hanno the imp waving his arms and jumping up and down with tears rolling down his face, chanting his final farewell ode to the Captain and the Hiker. We'll miss that old wacko, but not for a while!

Kermit gave us his card at the Georgetown Airport and told us to present it to his colleague at the El Greco Hotel on West Bay Street when we got to Nassau. And after saying our goodbyes to the Bahamian Host of the Year, Kermit Rolle, we jumped aboard the Bahamas Air, and 60 minutes later, with help from a fast-moving taxi from the Nassau Airport, I handed Kermit's card to James at the front desk of the Grec. What a port in an otherwise funky Nassau storm!

The Hotel El Greco is a loose-knit group of exquisite guest suites situated on several levels around a Spanish-tile deco swimming pool cold enough to shrink a Canadian's gonads

instantly, the perfect antidote to the 75°F Exuma Ocean in which we had been used to cavorting these past five days.

The suites overlooking the pool were spacious, clean and well decorated, with good, firm beds, a satellite TV, and tile bath. There was a lovely balcony over the pool, surrounded by flowering vines affording total privacy, of which the Captain and I took full advantage, smoking fat Cuban cigars and yelling at the NFL game all Sunday afternoon. In order to justify the pig-out in front of a television full of football games, we first hiked out the 3 miles along West Bay Street to the big bridge over Nassau Harbor to Atlantis Casino and Ocean Aquarium on Paradise Island. But having arrived at the gigantic fish prison, where all creatures breathing through gills were unhappily trapped in see-through plastic being observed by millions of snotty-nosed rich kids with their Versace moms and Nautica dads, we felt far too sad for the fish out of water to spend the $25 U.S. each. No sense encouraging the bastard merchants in this mad and tragic enterprise.

Sunday night it was "Home again, home again, jiggity jig," flying our way back to Toronto laden with gifts for the women. Katie wanted a necklace, Maryanne some earrings, Lucy a bracelet and Libby of course wanted nothing, so I got them each a bracelet of shells, golden earrings and necklaces from the sea — kind of buying my way back into their lives. It's the small price I pay for the occasional escape from the House of Women in which I live.

These Air Only Adventures are only thinly disguised as chapters in my book or reports on the radio station. I have been flying away on these junkets for as long as I can remember. There is something soul stirring and heart quickening about the idea of jumping on a plane with nothing but a small bag and a round-trip air ticket to somewhere I've never been before, without any concrete idea of where I'll end up, much less who I'll meet, and what they'll do with me once I get there.

If the idea stirs something within you, then buy a ticket, put some money in your pocket, and head out into the Big Blue. You'll feel better about the world and your place in it, I promise you.

By the way, Kermit's phone number is 242-345-0002 or 242-345-6038. It's $60 per room per night, or $30 each for two. The phone number of the El Greco Hotel is 242-325-1121, and the address is P.O. Box N-4187, Nassau, Bahamas. It's $85 per room per night for two. The International Youth Hostel is at 23 Delaney Street, at West Bay, Downtown Harbour, Nassau, and can be reached at 242-323-2904 (ask for Jeff Collins). The cost is $26 per night, double occupancy.

62 *Air Only Expeditions — Bahamas Taxi Man*

My old, dear acting coach, Sandy Meisner, used to say that we must adjust to the given circumstances in order to be successful actors. If, in an improvisation, your acting partner suggests that you are a locomotive, your very best response is "chug-a-chug-a-choo-choo." If, in life, someone hands you a bag of lemons, adjust to what you are given; make that lemonade, bunky, and throw a party. This ability to adjust will also serve you well in your travels.

I've always felt that the journey, along with the people you meet, is the true adventure when travelling, and a heck of a lot more fun for me than the holiday resort destination where we all cower behind those sturdy compound walls and the only locals you meet are the drug dealers and the sister sellers shouting to you over that wall. Most folks lock in their reservations for the places they'd like to stay, especially while travelling in a foreign country, for fear they'll be left out in the cold and dark with no place to go if they haven't booked a place ahead of time. Well folks, I have found that in most tropical countries, this predicament simply will not occur. Bahamian people, for example, are so damned friendly and open that they'll go out of their way to point you in the direction of all your desires, starting with, in most cases, a cozy and inviting guest cottage right on the beach, away from everybody, and normally at one third of the price you'll pay at a resort hotel. That's not too much to ask of Fortuna, the Goddess of Travellers. Especially

if you've been a good person lately. Have you been a good person lately?

So, here's how you go about planning your very own Air Only Expedition. Book tickets to someplace exotic you've always wanted to go. Put your ticket in your passport along with your driver's licence and a VISA card and some American dollars. Pack your bag very lightly (I've learned the hard way). Wear your nice clothes for travelling and clearing Customs, and pack an alternate outfit for hiking and swimming, one good book, a little radio, plastic rain poncho in a sack for the bottom of your bag, and a toothbrush.

The trick is to travel as lightly and quickly as you can, on and off the planes, so you don't have to wait for baggage at the airport carousel. This way you can clear Customs quickly and politely and head directly for the taxi stand. Now you're first in line, and you get your choice of taxi men. They'll all come up and hit on you. "Taxi, sir? Taxi, sir?" Here's what you do. Take your time. Choose carefully. Find the taxi man who is friendly, intelligent and closest to your age and generation. Don't panic. Be patient. Just smile and listen, and find the guy you like. He's the passport to your dream vacation requirements. Taxi man knows where everything is on the island, so when you're mobile, sit up front with him and strike up a conversation. When he asks you "Where to?" tell him that you're used to staying at a nice hotel (then name a hotel if you know one on the island. In our case it was the Peace and Plenty Hotel in Georgetown on the island of Great Exuma). But this time, tell him you're having your doubts about staying there, because you think it's too damned expensive, and you fear you're not going to get to know any of the local island folks, because that's why you came, to "jump up" with the local gang (which is "party down, dude" in Bahamian).

It's truly amazing how quickly the taxi man comes up with myriad alternatives for your humble consideration. That's how we met taxi man Kermit Rolle at the Exuma Airport in Georgetown. We'd mentioned the Peace and Plenty to him, a well-reputed, high-end sailor-and-sport-fisherman's haven, with great food and rooms ashore for the sea-going yachtsman. But I bemoaned the fact that we would probably

miss the villages and back roads if we stayed in the big town. And as I've already related to you, in an instant, Kermit suggested we come and stay at his family villa, unused except for the evangelistic, eccentric caretaker Hanno, and would we please use the hilltop sanctuary overlooking the sea as a base for our hiking forays into the local jungle and oceanside trails?

This good fortune happens far too often to be coincidence. The taxi man can make it happen for you, so choose carefully at the airport, find a taxi man you like, and you'll enjoy your stay. Taxi man will show you where the shops are, he'll introduce you to the fruit-and-veggie man, the fisherman who catches the grouper and lobster for your dining pleasure, and even the Rastaman for fresh herb, if you're that way inclined. Owning a taxi van on the islands is a sign of success; the driver is a man of authority and responsibility who commands respect. The taxi man makes people and equipment move from place to place cheaply and quickly. He'll get the doctor if you're ill, he'll drop off a bottle of rum just to be social, and stay for a drink to see how you're doing. He'll make suggestions for restaurants and "jump-up" parties around the island, and he'll make sure you and your luggage get back to the airport sober and ready for your plane ride home. Taxi man is your friend. He'll help make your Air Only Adventure a success.

SHERPA CORNER: Observations and Remarks from Hiker Mike's Crew

The following section contains reminiscences, ruminations and friendly advice from those wild and wacky hikers with whom I share the trail and my life.

63 *All in a Day's Work*

by Captain Karl Pruner

Algonquin Park. When I was growing up, those two words conjured up a whole world of wilderness adventure. Algonquin Park meant camping and canoeing, hiking and swimming, outdoor education and wildlife encounters. Like a lot of things that made a deep impression on me, I took it for granted that the Park would always be there, and I filed my plans for going back under the murky heading "Someday."

Well, hikers, "Someday" finally came when Hiker Mike turned up on the other end of my telephone line with a breathtakingly simple idea.

"Let's go hiking in Algonquin Park," says Hiker Mike.

"Great idea," I heard myself say.

And that is how, after a 40-year absence, I ended up at the trailhead of Booth's Rock Trail in Algonquin Park on a rainy day in October with my buddy and hiking mentor, Hiker Mike Kirby. Yes, hikers, I found out that you can get there from here and you can go there today. The moral of the story? Never put off until tomorrow the hikes that you put off yesterday.

Booth's Rock Trail: "There's nothing either good or bad, but thinking makes it so."

64 *Hand Me Down My Old Walking Stick*

by David Bradstreet

"Hand Me Down My Old Walking Stick," by Big Joe Williams, is one of a number of versions of this traditional song that speaks to the virtue of one of the oldest and dearest tools that mankind has ever invented — the walking stick.

So why is there so much resistance to this wonderful

innovation? Why, when coming upon a fellow hiker carrying a Moses rod, do the words "nerd," "dork," or just plain "dumb-lookin'" leap to mind for most North Americans? I really don't know, but I suppose it's a fashion thing, or fear of looking old in this perpetually youth-oriented culture. Whatever the reason, for the folks that have discovered its virtues, it's a heaven-sent hiker's companion.

A couple of years ago (has it really been that long?) I broke my hip. Not exactly the hell that Stephen King went through after being struck by a van, but serious nonetheless. I broke it in 10 pieces, and I now sport a few extra pounds of shiny stainless steel in my butt. My wife calls me the "Bad Ass Weatherman" because along with the obvious discomfort and the career-stalling effects, it gave me the uncanny ability to sense a change in the weather. Plus, it taught me how to use a cane! Cool.

Now I had one of those really neat fold-up ones. You know the kind that looks like a weapon sticking out of my backpack. That, along with the alarms at the airport security because of my bionics, raised the suspicions of the gun-toting border folks. Frankly, I was glad to see they were on their toes, though some of them could try poking and prodding with a little less glee. Of course, these days we are all very thankful for their diligent efforts. However, when the bells and whistles go off around me I take great pleasure in showing them the picture in my Palm Pilot of my posterior hardware and explaining "the weapon" away (because my family knows how to buy for me really nifty foldy things — I'm a gadget freak and proud of it!).

So after healing in record time, thanks largely to Hiker Mike who got me up and hiking again, I attempted to hit the comeback trail. Luckily I discovered the joys of the cane on these hikes. Now I had three legs! What balance and agility I discovered. What a handy stream-hopping device this truly is! It wasn't until our Urban Sherpa pal Captain Karl Pruner showed up one day with *two* walking sticks that I thought "to hell with the fashion gaff, if it's good enough for handsome Karl, it's good enough for me!" As he disappeared into the distant horizon, his stride double mine, I vowed to be a Stick Guy too. Not only just to keep up, but also to minimize the gear gap with Karl.

Now comes the technical stuff. . . .

After surrendering to the walking stick, I started the research. I was surprised to learn that a single walking stick can reduce the weight on your legs, hips and knees by 10 tons per hour! That's right, dear reader, no typo here — 10 tons an hour. Think about it. If you push down on the stick with, say, 5 pounds per step, at 60 steps per minute, that's 3,600 steps per hour and that's — okay that's 9 tons, but pretty good, eh wot? If you walk a bit faster and push a little harder, there's yer 10 tons! Okay, now multiply by two sticks and you have enough saved kinetic energy to pull a Range Rover out of a North African quicksand!

Now let's talk a bit about the balance and agility. For the skiers among you, I don't have to tell you that having four legs is better than two. Just watch Rupert the Malamute as he looks over a 200-foot cliff. My stomach is somewhere in my left ventricle as I watch him extend his head over for a peek, as he hangs ten on the edge. I realized on a recent trip to the Adirondacks with Mike that Rupert, though seemingly dangerously close to his maker, had the majority of his huge dog body still well planted on solid rock — clinging claws and all. In all my years of hiking with this great, pungent dog, I have never seen him fall over anything. The same cannot be said for poor ol' Tracker Dave or even Hiker Mike, for that matter — we are both on very intimate terms with face-rushing dirt.

I recall crossing a stream with another of our Urban Sherpa friends, Linda Sorensen. As daunting as rushing water can sometimes be, I have learned to surrender to the occasional soaker, taking it all in stride as it were. But Linda was determined not to get even a drop on her shiny new hiking shoes. Using a couple of fallen branches for balance, she deftly picked her way from boulder to boulder, with Mike and I cheering her on from the far shore. She made it gracefully, and as we continued on our trail we were serenaded by the squishing sound of our four wet male feet, with the counterpoint of Linda's soft percussion of two dry female ones. Another lesson learned, gender bashing aside.

So I now am the proud owner of a sparkling blue, collapsible walking stick. The next time you encounter a fellow hiker,

probably European, with his or her state-of-the-art hiking stick, remember, not only will you save wear and tear on your ambulatory gear and gain grace and balance, you are also getting one hell of an upper body workout in the process. I finally have the arms and shoulders of Jane Fonda.

So there you have it, folks. The Life-Saving, Body-Building, Soaker-Reducing, Third-Leg Balancing Act — walking stick!

Nerd or not.

65 *Walking Stick 2: Hiker Mike's Retort*

A couple of Saturdays back, I had the good fortune to be a part of the Bruce Trail Toronto Club's Annual General Meeting, after which I was allowed to stand in front of the entire hiking horde and create for them *The Living Map of Megacity Hiking*, in which I played all the parts myself: the parks, ravines and waterfront trails of Toronto, "the land between the rivers."

I placed the audience in Lake Ontario, and directly in front of them was the Martin Goodman Waterfront Trail moving from west to east, and along the top of the stage I placed the mighty Oak Ridges Moraine running from the Haltons and Caledons in the west to the Northumberland Hills east of Bowmanville. Then, like a giant ladder laying on the ground, I placed the rungs of all the Megacity rivers — the Duffins, the Rouge, Don, Humber, Etobicoke and Mimico Creeks and the beautiful Credit River running north to Belfountain and the magical land of Gitchi Manitou.

And for my trouble, the Bruce Trail Toronto Club rewarded me with a beautiful Castrock Stocke walking stick, makers of German hiking staffs since 1868. The wood has been grown and naturally aged for two years. The staff takes up to 25 percent of a person's weight off their knees and lower back and has a multi-use steel-spike tip for hiking and outdoor use, with an attachable rubber tip for use on rock or pavement. Mine is made of chestnut wood, long, slim, strong and shiny dark

brown, and I will treasure it till the day I die, when I will pass it to my Three Babes for their hiking forays.

Castrock Stocke is made by Mountain Properties, and their phone number in B.C. is 604-826-9699. Give them a call and they'll send you a catalogue. You won't regret it.

The walking stick has since saved my life, when high atop the Khumbu Glacier I moved off the trail to accommodate an oncoming herd of yak, only to lose my balance on the icy gravel, beginning to plummet to my death thousands of feet to the valley floor below. Jamming the metal point of the walking stick into the wall of ice, I managed to arrest my fall and pull myself to safety and back onto the trail in front of a dozen open-mouthed hikers, who then asked me where they could get a walking stick like mine.

66 *How to Pack a Backpack*

by Hiker Mike

When we hiked to Everest Base Camp, yaks and Sherpas carried our big hockey bags full of gear and supplies. All we carried were day packs containing extra socks, a book, a camera, our smokes and water and a Mars bar. Carry nothing but absolute essentials when you're hiking. Pack and unpack before you leave, until you are sure you can't live without the contents of your bag, or you'll be sorry. We're so damned insecure embarking upon a trip that we always carry too much. The secret is to carry nothing, but if you must, get Tracker Dave to carry it.

67 *Tracker Dave's Backpack*

by Dave Bradstreet

As a songwriter/sound recordist I carry some extra items in my day pack that perhaps wouldn't apply to most folks. But here is a partial list of what I would consider essential: a first-aid kit, a waterproof jacket, work-hiking gloves, CampSuds and a towel, a camera and film, a Swiss Army knife, a Leatherman Tool, 81 twine, a sewing kit, a compass, a watch, a MiniMag flashlight, sunglasses, glasses, AM-FM radio, extra underwear (doubles as a swimsuit), peaked cap, sunscreen-bug lotion, pepper spray (ya never know), wallet and keys, water, a magazine or novel, and pen and paper.

To this list I add a few extra clothes, digital recorder, cell phone, toilet paper and a few accessories like batteries, large green garbage bag (emergency rain cover), cash, important papers and passport. With all this stuffed into an Arc 1 Teryx Arro 22L pack, I'm ready to jump on a plane and head off to another world adventure with Hiker Mike! Total weight: 10 pounds!

I have found that by making a habit of always carrying a complete kit on my regular hikes and always having that extra 10 pounds with me, not only do I have my essentials, but I have managed to develop my upper body strength to the point that I really don't notice the weight anymore. As a matter of fact, I miss it when it's not there — my balance is not quite as tuned. It has also helped me to recover from a broken hip last year. As Mike used to say, "Hike two hours a day and carry ten pounds and we'll be hiking well into the sunset years."

68 *Toronto to Vancouver Hiking: Bi-Coastal Babe Boots the Beltline*

by Linda Sorensen

One sticky August day in 1987, my good buddy Mike Kirby suggested that I go for a walk with him. My response was something like, "Are you nuts! Why walk when we can drive in an air-conditioned vehicle?" But before I could say Mephisto, he had me hoofing it through a shady ravine in the heart of downtown Toronto.

How could I have lived here for 20 years and failed to realize that these pockets of tranquility are woven like ribbons throughout the entire city. All it took was that first walk through the cool, filtered forest air and I became Hiker Mike's

Pen Pal: Gestur from Iceland

"Dear Mike: I have been looking at your Internet site and have seen that you have praised the sole material of your Salomon hiking boots. I have been using the Salomon Super Mountain 9, the Snow and Ice version. The sole material which Salomon has selected is far from being the same quality and reliability as the upper part, and I can not see why they do not select the Vibram material, which for many years has been the best you can put under any hiking boots. In snow and ice, and believe me in Iceland you do see enough of it, the material has proven to be slippery and not reliable. Besides, it has not lasted very well, I have now had my boots resoled with Vibram and now I can tell you that the Salomon shoes are superb, possibly the best money can buy I might add. Please make this information available to your readers."

— *Sincerely, Gestur Valgardsson, Kopavogur, Iceland*

"I have had this complaint constantly from countless hikers, But let me say that I wouldn't be here with you today without my Salomon Extreme low-cut hikers. Several years ago I attempted a descent in which I lost control halfway down a 60-foot vertical, through no fault of my Salomons, which were gripping the loose jumble underfoot as best they could. I was running down the cliff, attempting to grab hold of trees to slow my fall, but nothing worked. No one was more surprised to find me standing at the bottom of the rocky river valley without one broken bone. The thanks for my survival must go to the Salomon grip. So there!" — *HM*

first "Urban Sherpa." The following is one of my favourite urban walks.

From Summerhill, where I live, I head west from the Cottingham School across Avenue Road. I then make my way through the Republic of Rathnelly, up Poplar Plains Road and over to Winston Churchill Park. Heading north, I eventually spill out onto St. Clair Avenue across from the big new Loblaws store. It's a little tricky here for Sherpas as there is no light on which to cross, so I exercise caution. Once accomplished, I find my way through to Heath Street, where the ravine picks up again just behind the Heath Street Subway Station. Now it's back down into the ravine and on up through Cedarvale Park with its abundance of dogs and tennis enthusiasts. I like to take this section at a good clip, booting it up to Eglinton Avenue as I work up a nice sweat. Again there is no light here, so I use caution in crossing.

Look for the tall sound barrier running along the east side of the Allen Expressway. There is a pathway running parallel to it, which will coax you north about two blocks to the well-marked "Beltline." Once on this abandoned railway line, I'm headed in a southeasterly direction. Walkers, joggers, cyclists and pooches enjoy this gracious tree-lined path, which eventually passes over Bathurst Street then Avenue Road and eventually to Yonge Street. Here I make the choice to head south on Yonge and back to Summerhill, or if time permits, to cross over Yonge Street and continue on through the Mount Pleasant Cemetery, always respectful of the dear souls resting therein. This route lures me south across Moore Avenue and plunges me down into the Rosedale Ravine, which leads me through Balfour Park and up the steep-staired incline to Summerhill Gardens. I'm almost home. Perhaps I'll stop at Patachou for a bowl of café au lait as I contemplate the lovely sensation deep within my muscles that results from a two-hour walk.

A note of caution: this Urban Sherpa never walks in the ravines alone, always with a buddy.

69 The Vancouver Sea Wall Walk

by Linda Sorensen

Walking has become like breathing for me, so I do it wherever I am. Vancouver is my second home, and every year I spend a few months here. My apartment is situated at the foot of Hornby Street, on the north side of False Creek between the Granville Street Bridge and the Burrard Street Bridge. I have a choice of many great urban walks right outside my front door. One of my favourites is the 5-mile Sea Wall Walk, which encircles Stanley Park plus another 3 miles back to my door.

In Vancouver, one must always be prepared for the inevitable rain. With the proper rain gear, walks are at the very least pleasantly refreshing. On a sparkling sunny day against a backdrop of snow-capped mountains, Vancouver walks are totally spectacular! As my apartment is literally on the sea wall, I begin my walk the minute I step out my front door. Heading north towards English Bay, I watch the seagulls sweep and scoop as they scavenge for scraps. I glimpse the sweet faces of sea otters and seals as they bob about in the harbour, sometimes lost and looking for a way back out to sea or perhaps just hanging around watching us humans. Small ferry boats resembling animated cartoons scurry about, taxiing tourists and shoppers back and forth to Granville Island. Dragon boats and kayaks glide gracefully through the chilly inlet waters, as huge barges piled with lumber demand the right of way. A plethora of sail boats, cabin cruisers and yachts venture in and out of their slips all day long. A brisk 10-minute walk and I'm at the English Bay Bath House. From here I continue along the beach, and within minutes I enter one of the world's finest parks.

Vancouverites know Stanley Park as "the lung of the city." Throughout the 1,000 acres of old-growth forest and fresh sea air are well-marked trails leading off to rose gardens, tennis courts, a pitch-and-putt golf course, saltwater pools, lighthouses and the Lost Lagoon, with its gushing fountain, boisterous ducks and arrogant swans.

I prefer to stay the course. An hour or so into my walk, I pass Siwash Rock, so graciously celebrated by the great Canadian poet Pauline Johnson. I clip past the slow walkers and baby strollers and soon glimpse the rusty underbelly of the Lions Gate Bridge. Heading towards Brockton Point with its stalwart lighthouse, a glance to my right reveals a grouping of majestic west-coast totem poles.

After rounding the point, I pass the Vancouver Yacht Club and head towards the Lord Stanley Monument, heralding the official entrance to Stanley Park. I'm now approximately 2½ hours from my door, and it's time to slip back through the streets of the west end to hook up again with the sea wall at English Bay. Here I have the choice of hoofing it back home or stopping at any one of the many eateries or coffee spots along Denman Street.

This is a good three-hour walk and one of the finest an Urban Sherpa will experience anywhere. Take it from Sherpa Linda, it's extraordinary!

70 *Sleepwalking*

by Chas Lawther

There are three hikes I've taken in my life to which I return again and again in my dreams. They're the familiar paths where I go for a walk as I fall asleep. Beginning at each trailhead, I can imagine each step of the way, every twist and turn, every view, every boulder, root and crevice.

The first is Capilano Canyon Park in North Vancouver, where I spent my teenage years hiking the trails. Whenever I go back out west, I always go to visit the trees and the river that were the companions of my youth. The last time I was there I took my sons, Joe and Isaac, who were 11 and 8. I showed them the small bridge I'd hidden under when I was chased by drunken high-school hooligans, and I almost pointed out the mossy bank where I shared my first kiss with Lynn Granger. Then the three of us stood together in silence on the rocky ledge overlooking the rapids where I'd seen a man fall out of his kayak and drown. I hope the boys, too, find trails so rich in adventure and memory.

My second sleepwalk is the one I took late one night in Vernon, B.C., up in the hills behind my sister's ranch. It was a full moon, so the trail was well lit and I knew it well, as it loops up and over the back hills of the Okanagan. After 10 minutes of walking, I'd adjusted to my fear that a serial killer was lurking behind every shadow and to the rustlings, grunts and barks surrounding me — they were only the sounds of creatures going about their nightly business. I was in a world of my own, absolutely alone — the only two-legged animal for miles and yet just another part of the outdoor night. On my way back, I descended into a small hollow surrounded by trees, shaded from the moon. Crossing the valley floor, it slowly dawned on me that I wasn't alone. I was being watched. I kept walking, but now my footsteps, instead of being just one part of the soundscape, were the only sound. I stopped, frozen with fear, unable to go on. As my eyes adjusted to the dark, I made out a shape about 10 feet from me, and then another and another, until I realized I was completely surrounded by cows, all of them standing stock still staring at me! A lifetime of filets, burgers and roasts flashed before my eyes. I hoped it didn't show on my face. We all just stood there silently until they finally let me go, after promising never to eat beef again. In my dreams, I still thank that ghostly bovine crowd for permitting me to continue hiking.

My third dreamwalk is one my wife, Gail, and I took in southern France a couple of years ago. We were in a tiny village called St. Guilhem-le-Desert. I could tell you its history, but since its centrepiece, the Abbey, was built in 776, you can understand that I don't really have the space in Mike's book. Late one sunny October afternoon, we walked through the village and wound our way up the back alleys until, by happenstance, we came on a footpath leading up the mountainside and eventually to the ruins of an 11th-century castle. Every step we took on that trail through the gorse, wild thyme and juniper had been taken by countless numbers through history. And as we got higher and higher, we seemed to move further back in time, until we could look all the way down the Verdus Gorge as it cut its way to the Mediterranean. When we got to the top and sat to take in the view, we gazed straight down into the village, hundreds of feet below, and watched the tiny figures of people as they lived their late-afternoon lives. The strange thing was that the acoustics were such that we could hear everything they said as clearly as if they were standing next to us. Their ancestors probably were!

Sometimes we sleepwalk together.

QUEST FOR THE HOLY TRAIL

71 *Speak the Speech I Pray You, Hiker Mike.*

Is there anybody out there who actually enjoys getting up in front of a roomful of people and saying a few words? Got a call from my old hiking pal Dan O'Reilly, one of the gurus behind the Humber Valley Heritage Trail. Dan, God bless him, asked me to do a chat and slide show for their annual general meeting, and a cold shiver shot up my backbone from coccyx to cranium. The thought of standing in front of a room full of hikers and talking about our sport was the equivalent of an invitation to my own hanging.

Everyone attending the meeting would be experienced woodsmen and women, all sitting there uncomfortably but quite on their best behavior, waiting for me to say something new and exciting about putting one foot in front of the other in fields far remote, somewhere out there on the Big Ball.

Hikers are normally singular and thoughtful individuals who take their private pleasure and refuge in the forests, at the lakeshore, in the mountains and in the parks and ravines, sharing their lonely lunch with whisky jacks and squirrels — not gathered together in an overly warm room, trying to be sociable and listening politely.

Hikers are like a herd of wild Shetland mustangs. Try to organize them and they'll eat you! "Whoa, hiker, slow down!" I steadied myself, realizing I always get paranoid at the idea of public speaking. "Whatever happened to Hiker Mike's credo of 'Yes to Everything!'?"

"Shame on you! Be a man! Snap out of it!" I shouted into the bathroom mirror. "Face your fears, you nervous Nellie." So I picked up the phone and made two calls, the first to Dan, accepting the invitation to speak, and the second to Joe Pilaar, who escorted me to Everest Base Camp once upon a time ago and with whom I shared a tent at 20,000 feet. I asked him if I could borrow his slides of the Everest Base Camp trek, all the way from Khatmandu to Gorak Shep and beyond to the Khumbu Glacier Ice Fields, where the climbers start to climb.

And Joey said, "Sure, man. No problem!" Now I feel much better. So sometime in March or April, I'll be standing in front of a bunch of hikers much like yourselves and giving my first slide show.

You see, gentle readers, I am in love not with public speaking, but with public property. Discovery hiking has always been a passionate adventure for me, especially when I'm following a foreign and potentially dangerous trail. I'm most comfortable when I'm firing information back at you, either in print or on the radio, as to where to go hiking, how to get to the trailhead and what you might see along the way. That's how I find I can best relate to my fellow outdoorsmen and women, not through the book signings, not through the hiking chats and certainly not through the slide-show sideshows.

Compared to these most self-consciously terrifying and confusing occasions, I must tell you that my upcoming colonoscopy is starting to look downright attractive. On the other hand, does anybody out there have a great hike you want me to go on? Tell me where and what time and I'll meet you at the trailhead in a Megacity minute. Hiker Mike's but a happy and hopefully healthy pilgrim on his never-ending Quest for the Holy Trail.

72 *Heading Back to Everest Base Camp — Spring 2001*

There is so much to do. I'd forgotten the gargantuan amount of prep involved in an expedition to the rooftop of the world. Of course there's the visit to the doctor for the countless inoculations: hep, typhoid, yellow fever, meningitis, polio and plague; the visit to my sponsors for the topping up of hiking gear such as LoweAlpine backpacks, Dunham Trail Triumph trek boots, SmartWool socks and underclothing; and then the journey downtown to MEC for a good reading light and water-purifying pills. But this time the trip preparations for Base Camp are tinged with new excitement and anxiety. This time, I will be leading the trek to the top. I will shoulder the responsibility for eight first-time trekkers who will look to me for answers, directions, band aids and reassurance that their quest through the thin air will end in success.

This whole outrageous idea of three-peating the Everest Base Camp Trek was born out of a winter's night dinner party, when my old friend Joe Pilaar came to our little cottage in Summerhill Gardens and brought with him the price of admission — his slide presentation of the Base Camp Trek. I had first seen the show in 1986, just before we set off to Kathmandu, in the Himalayan Kingdom of Nepal, to realize my lifelong dream of seeing the Earth Mother herself, Chomo Lungma.

The slideshow brought the joyous memories of the trek screaming back to me, and I found myself shouting over Joey's commentary with my own play-by-play, as the pictures familiar of temples, Sherpas, yaks and high mountain passes appeared on the screen. After the show, Joey said it was fairly apparent that the 15-year-old journey was still in my blood, and seeing as I felt that strongly about it, perhaps it was time that I do it again, but this time as trek leader.

And since all things are possible in the dinner party's rosy glow and the Yes to Everything philosophy was up there on the dinner table right beside the Beaujolais Villages, the 12-year-old idiot child inside my 55-year-old body responded immediately that "I'd be delighted and honoured to lead the springtime trek to Base Camp," quite possibly the most difficult and arduous hike found here on the Big Blue Ball.

That dinner party was five months ago, and now my flight leaves for Nepal in less than a week. I am quite candidly rife with anxiety, filled to the brim with self-doubt and fear and feeling new aches and pains that I swear were not apparent yesterday. My bones click and bang when I stand up and walk. My lower back rings alarm bells as I bend over. My Achilles tendon wants to be my Achilles tendon, as it seizes up when I try to get out of bed. My knees will not allow me to squat. My brain whispers, "Find a way out of this expedition bozo or I swear I'll kill ya. I mean it. You're too old to do this trip. The sherpas will be carrying you out in a basket. I'm warning you, I'll throw your goddamn back out like I did in Bahamas. You'll be a fool and laughingstock in front of all Toronto."

I've decided to try and hike my way, like a good ex-drunk, through the self-doubt by simply putting one foot in front of the other, one day at a time. Solve the simple problems as they arise, keep clearing the decks as I go. See what happens! Thankfully my schedule of "things to do" before jumping on the plane to Singapore doesn't allow me too much time to sit and think about the disaster scenarios that could befall me at every twist and turn on the high Himalayan trails leading to the Khumbu Ice Fall at 18,500 feet.

There have been tales of giant pack yaks goring trekkers over the cliffside of the pathway, leaving them screaming, bleeding while plunging into the bottomless abyss. I have seen trekkers sick from lack of oxygen who, while lying sobbing and shivering in their tents, could not even extricate themselves from their sleeping bags in order to eat or go to the bathroom.

I myself have felt the migraine axe smashing through my skull right between the eyes, and the inability to suck enough oxygen from the sky in order to satisfy my lung's mandate. I have done the two-holed glacier dance with poop and puke pouring forth profusely, while I could only laugh between spasms. But the worst I have seen is a trekker being carried unceremoniously down the mountain in a basket on the back of a tiny Sherpa porter.

That is the "humiliation ultime" that my brain keeps playing for me, like a revolving film clip at a dubbing session. I would rather die on the trail than be carried out in a basket. "That too," replies my brain, "is a distinct possibility."

Got an e-mail last week from Tory. It read, "My brother and I are thinking to do Base Camp Everest at the end of July. We want to do it without guides, following in the footsteps of Roy Orbison, using the only *The Lonely Planet Guide*. How bad is the monsoon there during this time? Is it unbearable? Is there much chance of snow during August? Any help appreciated. "

After I stopped laughing out loud, I picked up the phone and called my Himalayan hiking pal. If anybody would know about monsoon hiking in Nepal, it's Joe. And you know what he said?

"Sure, Tory, go ahead, you can hike the Himalayas in July. Just be sure to take plenty of Gore-Tex, because you'll be hiking underwater. And also you may never see any mountains because the river valley approach is totally shrouded in clouds. But once you're up the Khumbu Valley north of Namche Bazaar and Tangboche Monastery, above the treeline, you'll only get afternoon rain, as opposed to the all-day torrents further down the valley. If you're used to hiking Canada's west-coast trails, you'll feel right at home. The rains are so strong at times that the river will take half a mountain with it down the valley, and wipe out entire villages. Just so you can put the monsoon in perspective."

The best summer hiking is just to the west of northern India–Pakistan area in Ladakh, but getting there is a problem. There's a little animosity brewing between the old arch enemies, so you'll have to keep your head down from time to time, what with the artillery shooting at the helicopters and war planes shelling the villages closest to the army encampments. But a little further west in Ladakh, you're up on the Tibetan Plateau. It's desert area, very dry in the rain shadow, and the hiking is great. Joe hikes year-round in the Himalaya Annapurna Sanctuary, Everest Base Camp, Ladakh, so he's our man in Nepal, north India and Pakistan.

Nancy Reimer just sent me a "*Namaste*" from St. Catharines. That's "Hi, how are you?" in Nepalese. She called with questions about hiking up from Khatmandu to the Everest Base Camp just below 20,000 feet. Can she walk all the way without flying into Lukla?

Sure, I said. Just takes longer, is all. After leaving the cozy confines of the Khatmandu Guest House buried deep in the heart of Thamel, the student district, the best route is straight up the Dud Kosi River through Sherpa country to the beginnings of the Great Khumbu Glacier, just above the slag line, then on to Gorak Shep. Kala Pataar, the little mountain in the centre of a frozen lake, affords the hiker the absolute best 360-degree panorama of all the biggest 8,000-metre-plus Himalayan monsters, including Lhotse, Nuptse, Everest, Tam Serku and Ama Dablam.

Most Everest trekkers don't know any better and let the tour operators sell them on the idea of flying into Lukla and the Sir

Edmund Hillary Airport at 2,800 metres and beginning the trek from there. This is a big mistake, first because it'll cost you $300 U.S. for a 20-minute flight, and second, your body will not acclimatize to the distinct lack of oxygen for the remainder of the climb, so you'll be sick with nausea, headache, and heart-pounding for the journey to the Base Camp. Take it from Hiker Mike, the way to go is to walk in from Jiri, just outside Khatmandu.

You can take the bus from Kathmandu to the Jiri trailhead for five bucks and spend the next eight days tromping happily through the rice paddies, the rhododendron and pine forests, and little lowland sherpa villages until you reach Lukla fully acclimatized and ready for the extremely arduous journey ahead. Also, what most trekkers fail to realize is that you don't walk straight up the side of Everest from the lowlands of Khatmandu, like you do on Kilimanjaro in Africa, but up and down over a series of foothills, each mountain range rising progressively higher, until you descend behind the Buddhist temples of Tangboche and step onto the Khumbu Glacier, just above Dughla. Then it's pretty much straight up through the ragged little villages of Lobuche and Gorak Shep. If you go alone, man or woman alike, it's best to hire a porter guide to carry your bag and cook for you — about $50 U.S. a day — or you can carry your own damn bag and stay in the little restaurant lodges along the way. Much cheaper, but women must wear long skirts and travel in pairs, otherwise the local riffraff consider you a North American floozy in shorts with loose morals and will want to jump on you for sport.

If you're an independent and adventurous hiker like myself who enjoys discovering on your own or with a porter guide, call Joe Pilaar, my pal at Canadian Himalayan Expeditions, at 416-360-4300. He knows all the Sherpas who'll safely hike you to Base Camp. Either way, make sure you walk in from Khatmandu or else the lack of oxygen will have you dancing and emitting unattractive secretions from both ends of your spectrum simultaneously. And that, my friends, isn't any fun. Take it from one who's been there!

IN CLOSING

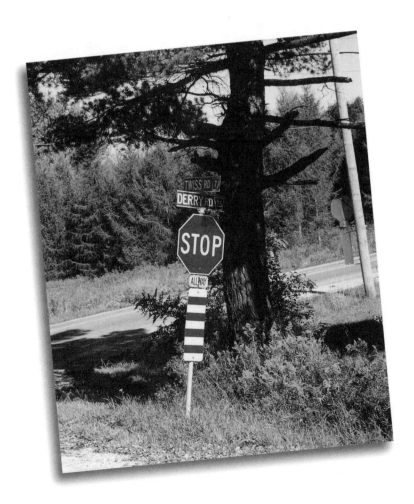

Pen Pal Angst

"Hey, Mike: I just bought your book *Hiker Mike's Best Hikes*. I want to thank you for the great book. I am an avid hiker, and until now I had been relying on undetailed hiking trail info from the local Travel and Tourism Authority.

"I do have one question for you. Where is the Golden Boot Award Hike? Number 50 in your book. I drove for two hours around Goodwood and could not find it. It took me a while to find the 3rd Concession, which after asking one of the locals I was told was Front Street.

"Secondly, the only gate on the right-hand side I could find turned out to be on private property! (After the owner inquired as to what I was doing on his property.) I also could not find Hyla's Farm as a landmark.

"Finally, where would one park? The concession road has no shoulders. Any suggestions?" — *Fellow Hiker*

I'm often castigated by hikers who e-mail me complaining that they cannot find the trailhead for the Goodwood Trail. I don't know why this is. Whenever I'm out in the Moraine between Stouffville and Uxbridge, I go and check my directions to Goodwood, and they always seem right to me. So let me try it one more time.

Goodwood Trailhead. Here is a sure-fire method of finding what can be easily called the finest Oak Ridges Section of trail in the Moraine. Take the Bloomington Sideroad to the little village of Goodwood. Make a right-hand turn and head south on Front Street, which turns into 3rd Concession Uxbridge. If you travel exactly 3.4K, you will see on the right side of the road an old, bent, metal farmer's gate, which sits beside two giant oak trees. On the fence post are two white Oak Ridges trail blazes, and the farmer's lane heads west into the fine conservation area, which happens to be the source of the Duffins. Now you hikers will be able to find Goodwood, winner of the Golden Boot Award for Best Toronto Hike 2000.

THANK YOUS

There is no one to whom I am more in debt for the completion of this book than the beautiful Elizabeth Lennie, who once again took the time to make some sense out of my longhand meanderings and type it all into our auld Mac Apple. Eliz also acted as my conscience in matters of taste, as I have been known to venture down that vulgar road more than once. My darling partner has managed to run the family business, keep both house and children clean, and conduct her own acting career while I have been in and out of the forest pretending to be hard at work writing a book.

Without my Urban Sherpas I would have no one to share my adventures, men and women like myself who think nothing of rising before dawn and hitting the Comeback Trail to Adventure, hiking all day with no more reward than a large regular coffee from Tim's. Two-time Genie-award-winning actress Linda Sorensen; singer-songwriter and old folkie Juno-Award-winner Tracker Dave Bradstreet, who knows more about hiking gear than Sherpa Tenzing; Capt'n Karl Pruner, film and television star, who lights up the trail with his scintillating mind; Beachman Gary with the kind heart and generous spirit, who can't stop talking about termites and technology, nature and humanity; and Stormy Blake, who rode shotgun down to the Adirondacks, my oldest and bestest pal. Thanks for keeping me company on those cold and dark mornings.

Thank you, dear friend John Donabie, weekend morning radio host to whose wonderful show I report every Saturday and Sunday. Always happy and positive and lovely to talk to, John has quietly insisted for five years that room must be made for Hiker Mike's outdoor blather at 8:20 AM, rain or shine.

Thanks to Michael Mayzell, whose LoweAlpine hiking gear and Lowe Pro photo gear found its way all over my body; and Clarence Rosevear, who keeps my feet warm and cozy with his Dunham New Balance boots.

Thank you, hiking buddy and ever faithful companion Rupert the Malamute, who has been with me on the trail for 13 solid years. May you hike on in heaven throughout eternity, my dear old animal friend.

Thank you, Maryanne, Lucy and Katy for coming on hikes with your old dad when no one else would. And to you, my editor, Jane Gates, thank you for turning all of this into a silk purse.